THE BEGGARS OPERA

BY

JOHN GAY

EDITED BY

Benjamin W. Griffith, Jr.
Mercer University

ILLUSTRATIONS

BY

Keogh

BARRON'S EDUCATIONAL SERIES, INC.
New York • London • Toronto • Sydney

All inquiries should be addressed to:
Barron's Educational Series, Inc.
250 Wireless Boulevard
Hauppauge, New York 11788

PRINTED IN THE UNITED STATES OF AMERICA

Library of Congress Catalog Card Number: 61–18353

89   510   20 19 18 17 16 15 14 13

THE PLAYWRIGHT

It was characteristic of writers in the eighteenth century to cater to the spirit of their age, but no writer reflected as many contemporary literary fashions as did John Gay. This amiable satirist wrote mock heroics, *vers de société,* pastorals, essays in the Addison and Steele manner, several of the few really fine lyrics of his day, fables, ballad operas, tragedies, and comedies. He penned three of the most popular works of the period: *The Beggar's Opera,* by all odds the most beloved play of the century; *The Fables,* of which there have been over 350 editions; and *Trivia,* which went into five editions during the poet's lifetime and which is generally acclaimed as the greatest poem ever written on London life.

But John Gay virtually has been overlooked when the literary laurels were handed down, and, curiously enough, this lack of critical favor is in part due to his positive genius for making friends. He was a close companion to Jonathan Swift and Alexander Pope, and it is as a friend of these giants of literature that he is most often given recognition. W. H. Irving entitled his excellent biography *John Gay, Favorite of the Wits* in deference to this manner of assessing the playwright. James Sutherland points out that "Gay's own friends rarely asserted his claims as a poet. They thought of him, and when he was dead they remembered him, as a man— gentle, good-natured, indolent, lovable in the extreme, shiftless, impracticable, innocent, volatile, a sort of Augustan Peter Pan riding in the coaches of his noble friends, dining at their tables, shooting their pheasants, but quite incapable of attending to his worldly affairs." But Gay was more than a lovable lapdog to his temperamental and sometimes difficult companions. He gave a good part of himself to his friends and was always ready to drop one of his schemes to assist with one of theirs and to give of his time and affection unstintingly. Pope's famous epitaph for his friend Gay was a sincere and fitting tribute:

> Of manners gentle, of affections mild;
> In wit, a man; simplicity, a child:
> With native humour temp'ring virtuous rage,
> Form'd to delight at once and lash the age:
> Above temptation, in a low estate,
> And uncorrupted, ev'n among the great:
> A safe companion, and an easy friend,
> Unblamed through life, lamented in thy end.
> These are thy honours! not that here thy bust
> Is mix'd with heroes, or with kings thy dust;
> But that the worthy and the good shall say,
> Striking their pensive bosoms—*Here* lies GAY.

Another side of the complex personality that was Gay's is found in the well-known epitaph—written by the playwright himself:

> Life is a jest; and all things show it.
> I thought so once; but now I know it.

Gay had written this saucy epigram some years before, and, during his serious illness of 1729, he wrote to Pope, requesting that it be placed on his tomb. When Gay's monument was unveiled on May 1, 1733, many persons were shocked at the frivolity of the inscription. Gay would have been surprised at this reaction, for he had indeed been destined to play jester to the world. He knew that his greatest contribution had been the supplying of gaiety to his fellows. He knew too well that his efforts to be other than a jester had all ended in frustration and disappointment.

To relate that the jester Gay was born on Joy Street smacks of a great cosmic joke. But so it was; on June 30, 1685, Gay was born at that address in Barnstaple, Devonshire. Although the Gays of Devonshire were of moderate means—some were poor parsons, some soldiers, some tradesmen—there was a tradition of family gentility. John Gay was the youngest son of a youngest son, but he could point proudly to a coat of arms on both halves of his family tree. In the large house on Joy Street Gay was apparently blessed with a happy early childhood. His hometown of Barnstaple was a large trading center, and, though it was seven miles upriver, had a considerable foreign trade in woolens and tobacco. Gay and his friends must have been interested in the exotic stories the sailors told down at the quay. Also Gay may have heard some tales from his Aunt Martha that would greatly influence his later life. His aunt, who had lost a fortune in a New World business venture, had been sent to Newgate Prison as a debtor for two or three years. Young John was later to use Newgate Prison as the setting for his most famous work, *The Beggar's Opera*. Although there was not a regular theatre in Barnstaple until 1768, the town supported what plays it could get, whether the actors were strollers or the traveling company of King's players. Also, Gay's schoolmaster, the Reverend Robert Luck, was a brilliant young High Churchman who wrote poetry and produced an annual Grammar School play. Schoolmaster Luck also insisted that Gay and his fellow students learn their classical languages, having them translate Latin verse into English. It was here that Gay's interest in poetry was kindled.

In 1694, however, life began to change for John Gay. In that year both his parents died—first his mother, and a few months later, his father—and an uncle, Thomas Gay, was given the responsibility of rearing the rather intractable ten-year-old boy who was given to carving his name on church pews. Seven years later Gay's uncle died, and the boy set out for London. Through the auspices of a cousin, Hester Pinney, who owned a lace shop, John was placed as an apprentice to a silk mercer on the Strand. William Ayre, in his *Memoirs of the Life and Writings of Alexander Pope, Esq.* (1745), gives a contemporary account of Gay's activities as an apprentice: "The Trade which he chose to be put Apprentice to, was a Mercer, but he grew so fond of Reading and Study, That he frequently neglected to exert himself in putting off Silks and Velvets to the Ladies, and suffer'd them (by reason of his wanting to finish the Sale in too few Words) to go to other Shops." Apparently Gay's interest in literature continued to interfere with his salesmanship, for in the summer of 1706, with only half of his apprenticeship completed, he was released by his master.

He went to Barnstaple temporarily, but he returned to London in 1707, where he obtained a post as secretary to Aaron Hill, a wealthy young dabbler in literature who was later to manage the Drury Lane Theatre for a short time. Hill, well known among coffeehouse literati, was Gay's entree into the society of London's wits and writers. Hill also helped Gay publish his first poem, *Wine* (1708), a rather artificial imitation of Milton. Gay had it printed in folio on expensive paper and was much annoyed when a pirated edition of the poem was published immediately on "brown sheets and scurvy letter." He was not annoyed, however, that the poem was considered important enough to be pirated.

Little is known of Gay's life from 1708–1711, but by the latter date the young aspirant to literary greatness had established a firm friendship with a true potentate of letters: Alexander Pope. It was Pope who encouraged Gay to turn his talents to the theatre, and in 1712 Gay published *The Mohocks,* a farce about a group of aristocratic young delinquents, named after a ferocious Indian tribe, who terrorized London by night. The play is marred by forced and somewhat derivative comedy. It is notable only for the well-delineated pictures of London streets and the molls, mountebanks, cinder wenches, watchmen, and ballad singers that inhabited them. The farce was never acted, but it helped to establish Gay with the literary clique of Pope, Thomas Parnell, and Nicholas Rowe.

Gay also tried his hand at pamphleteering during this period, but he had no real taste for it. Englishmen took their political pamphlets seriously in those days. Early eighteenth-century society was a seething arena of po-

litical strife, with the Whigs and Tories sitting on oppo-
site sides of theatres and beautiful ladies displaying their
party affiliations by special codes of wearing their
beauty patches. As Gay described the situation in the
poem *Rural Sports* (1713):

> Faction embroils the World; and ev'ry Tongue
> Is fraught with Malice, and with Scandal hung:
> Friendship, for Sylvan Shades, does Courts despise,
> Where all must yield to Int'rest's dearer Ties;
> Each Rival *Machiavel* with Envy burns,
> And Honesty forsakes them All by turns;
> While Calumny upon each Party's thrown,
> Which Both abhor, and Both alike disown.

In 1713 Gay at last found a sense of direction for his
literary energies. One of the reasons for the sudden find-
ing of himself was his employment as secretary to the
Duchess of Monmouth in the last months of 1712. The
sixty-two-year-old duchess, witty and good-natured,
lived the life of a *bon vivant* in a mansion in Chelsea.
Gay was now well situated, and his circle of friends at
Will's and Button's coffeehouses was growing. He now
had no financial worries, and the light routine of work at
the mansion left him plenty of time for writing. Gay took
advantage of his good fortune; the poem *Rural Sports*
appeared on January 13, 1713; a play, *The Wife of
Bath,* was produced on May 12; and a poem, *The Fan,*
was ready for publication on December 8. *Rural Sports*
is a descriptive poem, noted chiefly for the original con-
cept of introducing country sports into the framework of
a georgic. *The Wife of Bath* was unsuccessful; it ran for
only three nights, and Gay referred to it later as his
"damned" play. It hardly deserved any better, for it was
a hopeless potpourri of ingredients borrowed brazenly
from Chaucer, Farquhar, and Shakespeare. *The Fan,*
although it was popular in the eighteenth century, is
really little more than an ineffective and overly deco-
rated retelling of Ovid's tales.

Although it was not completed in the year 1713, the

poem *The Shepherd's Week* was largely written during this *annus mirabilis*. The poem is a pastoral with
a difference, for Gay broke with the ridiculous Arcadian
tradition of nymphs and swains and sought to copy the
simplicity of Theocritus. Although the pastoral form had
been tried by all the young poets, including Pope, it was
Gay, as usual, who came up with a new approach. Pope,
in a facetious letter to Swift, speaks of Gay's efforts, calling the poet "an unhappy youth, who writes pastorals
during the time of divine services; whose case is the
more deplorable, as he hath miserably lavished away all
that silver he should have reserved for his soul's health,
in buttons and loops for his coat." *The Shepherd's Week*
was published on April 15, 1714, and became immediately popular, going into three editions the first year of
publication. Gay's pastoral brings the English village to
life, with vivid pictures of country games, wakes, and
fairs. The "Saturday" portion of the poem, with tipsy
Bouzybeus singing his songs, dancing among the merry
reapers, and kissing the girls, received the most popular
acclaim. The work received a great critical acclaim also.
Robert Shiels in 1753 wrote: "Of all Gay's performances, his Pastorals seem to have the highest finishing;
they are perfectly Doric; the characters and dialogue are
natural and rurally simple; the language is admirably
suited to the persons, who appear delightfully rustic."
Oliver Goldsmith praised Gay highly, stating that he
"has hit the true spirit of pastoral poetry. In fact, he
more resembles Theocritus than any other English pastoral writer whatsoever."

Also in 1713 Gay became secretary to the well-known
Scriblerus Club, which included the leading wits of the
day: Swift, Pope, Thomas Parnell, Dr. John Arbuthnot,
and Joseph Spence. As Spence stated the Club's purpose,
it was "to ridicule all the false tastes in learning." Under
the pseudonym of Martin Scriblerus, the Club was to attack pedantry on all fronts. Gay enjoyed the Club's activities more on a social than a literary level, and apparently there was a great deal of pleasure to be derived

from the association. Goldsmith described the Club as "a society, in which, of all others, a wise man might be most foolish without incurring any danger of contempt." The Club was active from November, 1713, to June, 1714, when, for various reasons, the group became separated.

The year 1714 was a difficult one for Gay. He had been extremely fortunate in the friends he had made, but his literary success was limited to one poem: *The Shepherd's Week*. He now sought a political office that would provide him the wherewithal to live among the literary society he loved. He soon obtained the post of secretary to Lord Clarendon, who was heading a Tory public relations mission to Hanover. Clarendon, a poor choice in any public relations venture, had served as governor of New York and had been the laughing stock of the colonists when he appeared at state functions dressed as a woman in order to represent the Queen more exactly. Gay, however, made the most of his travels on the Continent from late June to the middle of September. The late months of 1714 he spent in attempting to cultivate court acquaintances and in writing *The What d'ye Call It,* a farce that was to be produced at Drury Lane the following February.

The What d'ye Call It was Gay's first theatrical success. He made a hundred pounds from it, and it was acted twenty-two times during the first two seasons and revived in almost every season until 1750. The farce was considered by many to be a new kind of play. The primary focus of it is literary burlesque, specifically directed against the tragedies of the day. So subtle was the parody that many of the patrons took the work seriously and found cause for weeping. A high point in the production was the beautiful ballad beginning, " 'Twas when the seas were roaring," set to music supposedly written by Handel. The ballad has had a long-standing success apart from the play, having been reprinted down through the years. This ballad not only demonstrates Gay's gifts as a lyricist—a rare talent in the eighteenth century—but it also points ahead to the songs which were to enliven *The Beggar's Opera.*

Gay spent the remainder of 1715 in attempting to procure a post at Court and in completing the poem *Trivia*, which was published on January 26, 1716. *Trivia,* subtitled "The Art of Walking the Streets of London," is unquestionably the greatest poem on London life in English literature. Filled with vivid and varied detail, the poem describes at least sixty ways of earning a living and more than thirty-five separate London locales. The poem is divided into three parts: the first sets out the implements for walking, and the latter two describe walking by day and by night. Throughout the work Gay is burlesquing classical forms and classical similes. The poem went into five editions during the author's lifetime and proved again that Gay was a master at inventing literary schemes and attracting the public with them. The poem was also a financial success. Arbuthnot commented that "Gay has got so much money by his Art of Walking the Streets, that he is ready to set up his equipage," meaning, of course, that Gay could now afford a carriage and horses.

Gay was soon involved with Pope and Arbuthnot in the writing of a satirical comedy, *Three Hours After Marriage.* Gay contributed the original idea as well as the structural organization of this farce, which was little more than a catch-all for the personal grudges of these three members of the Scriblerus Club. Three rival writers—Josiah Woodward, John Dennis, and Colley Cibber —are satirized in the play through the characters: Fossile, Sir Tremendous, and Plotwell. Because of the strength of the literary factions then in London, a riot occurred on the opening night (January 16, 1717) and recurred through the seven nights of its run. Perhaps because of its notoriety, the play had a longer run than any other play that season, and the playhouse was full at every performance. Another reason for its popularity was the fact that the pious Joseph Addison had charged that the play was obscene. The play was a source of much embarrassment for Gay, and the forty-three pounds and odd shillings he received for the copyright was little enough recompense.

Gay spent much of 1718 and 1719 in traveling and in visiting his friends. In November, 1719, he returned to London after a trip to the Continent; he was badly in need of money. In an effort to improve his finances he wrote *Dione,* a pastoral tragedy now virtually forgotten. It was not accepted for theatrical production, but was published in the collected edition of Gay's poems in 1720. In August, 1720, Gay was working with several other lyricists on songs for Handel's first English oratorio, *Queen Esther.* He was also suffering a severe financial loss at this time through ill-advised investments in stock of the infamous South Sea Company. Now in dire financial straits, Gay's lot continued to worsen until the spring of 1723, when he was given a commissionership of state lotteries at 150 pounds a year. At this time the Earl of Lincoln obtained lodgings for Gay at Whitehall.

Assured of a steady income and a place to live, Gay now found time to turn to further ambitious literary schemes, the first of which was a conventional poetic tragedy, *The Captives.* This play has all of the stock accoutrements, including a noble hero, the sentimental tyrant, and the love-maddened princess, held together with the scantiest of plots. With its stilted, florid blank verse and its many clichés, it is exactly the sort of play Gay had lambasted in *The What d'ye Call It.* Queen Caroline was interested in the play, however, and requested that Gay read it to her at Leicester House before it was staged. An embarrassing incident occurred at the reading: the corpulent Gay tripped over a footstool as he bowed to the Queen and fell onto a large screen, overturning it. And there was more embarrassment yet to come. When the play was opened on January 15, 1724, at Drury Lane, a custom was followed whereby the play was "christened." This christening took the form of distributing large quantities of brandy to the footmen in the boxes. Many of these footmen were later carried from the playhouse dead drunk. Although the play ran only seven performances, the published version went into two editions in as many months.

Not being satisfied with his small annual salary, Gay continued to seek Court preferment. In December, 1725, he was able to combine his aspirations as a courtier with his ambitions as a writer; he began composing *The Fables* for the Princess Caroline's four-year-old son, Prince William Augustus. *The Fables,* which were finished by October, 1726, and published in March, 1727, bore an inscription indicating that they were written for the little Prince's amusement, but almost every reader in England was soon to share in the pleasure. The fable was a popular literary form of the period, but Gay's bold addition of still another work in the genre was amply rewarded. There have been over 350 editions of the work, most of them before 1890, and the book was widely used as a text in elementary schools for over a hundred years. Gay's epigrams and stories soon became household words. This is despite the fact that the "morals" in the original fifty tales of the first edition concern only the courtier; many of them warn young Prince William of the dangers of flattery and sychophancy. The verses are witty and well turned, as exemplified by Gay's reference to himself in the last fable:

> A Hare, who, in a civil way,
> Comply'd with everything, like *Gay*,
> Was known by all the bestial train,
> Who haunt the wood, or graze the plain:
> Her care was, never to offend,
> And ev'ry creature was her friend.

Gay's efforts to win Court favor met with little success. In October, 1727, when the list of preferments appeared, Gay was appointed Gentleman Usher to the two-year-old Princess Louisa, a post worth a mere 150 pounds a year. Gay, feeling that he was selling his allegiance to the Court party at too small a figure, promptly declined the position. In a letter to Swift, explaining his decision, Gay stated that his freedom from Court entanglements would leave the way open for the production of *The Beggar's Opera,* a harsh satire on Walpole and Townshend. The basic satirical strain in the play implies, of course, that the rogues and thieves of Newgate operate in much the same way as those who run the government. *The Beggar's Opera* opened on January 29, 1728, to unprecedented applause and acclaim.

After this great theatrical success, Gay found himself surrounded by friends. He was financially secure, but his means were never more than moderate, and he found it increasingly difficult to resist the temptation to keep up with his extravagant companions. He spent the warm months of 1728 at Bath, but he continued to work at his writing. By November, when he suffered an attack of fever, he had nearly completed *Polly,* a sequel to *The Beggar's Opera.* Attempting to cash in on the public favor of its predecessor, Gay rushed *Polly* to the boards, but in December he received the first hint that the sequel was to meet with many obstacles. At that time John Rich, the theatrical producer, received orders from the Lord Chamberlain to delay rehearsals of *Polly* until further notice. The Lord Chamberlain was in error in assuming that *Polly* was as politically dangerous as *The Beggar's Opera.* The satire in the sequel is much blunted by Gay's transferring of the action from Newgate to a colonial plantation. Many of the attacks on flattery and insincerity seem inappropriately carried over from the preceding play. Macheath, in the sequel, is disguised as a Negro and is not at all presented as the hero who won all hearts in *The Beggar's Opera.* Polly has become a cardboard cliché, a mere reworking of the sentimental heroine type; she finally marries an Indian lover. The ballads, far beneath Gay's previous standards, are irregular and seem hastily contrived. Perhaps it is for the best that

the Lord Chamberlain prohibited the production of
Polly and that it did not come to the stage until nearly
fifty years after Gay wrote it. When the Lord Chamberlain's final decision to suppress *Polly* was announced on
December 12, 1728, however, a great furor arose.
Everyone who had a grievance against the government
took up Gay's *cause célèbre* against this censorship.
Although Gay suffered a severe attack of fever, pleurisy,
and asthma in late December, he made plans to continue the fight by publishing the play, along with a
preface to defend his position. A subscription list was
started, and one of Gay's truest friends, Kitty Hyde, the
Duchess of Queensberry, took the subscription list to
Court and added names under the very eyes of the
King. For this she was dismissed from the Court. The
subscription list filled rapidly; Henrietta, Duchess of
Marlborough, subscribed 100 pounds for a single
copy. The final list totaled 1,200 pounds.

Most of the rest of 1729 was spent idly on junkets
with the Duke and Duchess of Queensberry to Scotland
and to their ancestral home in Oxfordshire. What little
literary energy Gay could muster was spent in revamping
an earlier theatrical failure, *The Wife of Bath*. When it
was presented at Lincoln's Inn Fields on January 19,
1730, it was again a failure despite Gay's revisions. That
year he spent a pleasant summer with the Duke and
Duchess of Queensberry at their summer house in Ames-
bury. There he played with the children, shot quail on
Salisbury Plain, and amused himself by laughing at the
duchess's experiments in milking cows. He wrote little,
telling Swift in a letter that since the doctors had forbid-
den him wine, no poetry should be expected of him.
More likely, however, Gay was too contented in his in-
dolence to turn back to writing.

Gay returned to London for about ten weeks in
the winter of 1730–31 with his health apparently much
improved. In March he supervised the first London
performance of *Acis and Galatea* in Lincoln's Inn
Fields. Gay had written this little operetta to Handel's

music ten years earlier. In the summer of 1731, **Gay** was searching for a suitable writing project; he finally decided on a continuation of *The Fables*. But Gay, whether because of his tendency to ill health or because of his laziness, found it difficult to work. Swift wrote him, chiding his lack of literary production: "You mortally hate writing, only because it is the thing you chiefly ought to do; as well to keep up the vogue you have in the world, as to make you easy in your fortune. You are merciful to everything but money, your best friend, whom you treat with inhumanity. Be assured I will hire people to watch all your motions and to return me a faithful account." Gay replied by outlining his literary activities. He was then completing the second series of *The Fables* and making plans for the new opera, *Achilles,* which was written during the summer of 1732.

In both of these works there is a recurrent strain of bitterness against the Court. The disease that was to take Gay's life was daily taking a greater toll of his energies, and in this weakened condition his frustrations and ill feelings toward corrupt politicians and courtiers came to the forefront. In *Achilles* there is much said about the duplicity of those in high places. The second series of *The Fables* repeats the refrain, adding a number of thrusts at the politicians. Gay's sense of injustice became an *idée fixe*. Two other plays, *The Distress'd Wife* and *The Rehearsal at Goatham,* were written during the last year or two of Gay's life, but published posthumously. These plays also show an embittered, ill Gay striking out against the futility of office-seeking and the necessity of toadying to the great and near-great. Thus the gentle, loving Gay had become a cynic, capable of slashing out at the politician in the later *Fables* in this manner:

> I see him, mad and drunk with power,
> Stand tott'ring on ambition's tower:
> Sometimes, in speeches vain and proud,
> His boasts insult the nether crowd:

> Now, seiz'd with giddiness and fear,
> He trembles lest his fall is near.

In mid-November, 1732, Gay came to London to make arrangements to put *Achilles* in rehearsal at the Covent Garden. Within two weeks he was mortally ill. His friend Dr. Arbuthnot and two other physicians worked valiantly to save his life; but on December 4, three days after the illness struck, Gay died. Arbuthnot wrote to Swift that Gay's attack—diagnosed as inflammation of the bowels—was the most precipitate case he had ever seen. Pope and Arbuthnot wrote to Swift, who had a strange premonition that the letter contained bad news. He refused to open it until five days later. Swift's answer, written in an attitude of quiet mourning, stated that "in a few days past, two persons of great merit, whom I loved very well, have died in the prime of their years, a little above thirty." Lord Bathurst, in expressing his grief, made a statement that might have been echoed by many others: "Poor John Gay! We shall see him no more; but he will always be remembered by those who knew him, with tender concern."

The body lay in state at Exeter Change until December 23 and was then buried in Westminster Abbey beside the tomb of Chaucer. The Duke and Duchess of Queensberry had an elaborate monument erected for their friend, the monument including a bust by Rysbrock and Pope's famous epitaph. Also inscribed on the monument was the little couplet which Gay had referred to as "My Own Epitaph":

> Life is a jest; and all things show it.
> I thought so once; but now I know it.

Although many were shocked by Gay's levity even in death, those who knew him best found no cause to complain. To this gentle, lovable man life had indeed been a jest. And being the jester to the world had been a serious business for John Gay.

THE PLAY

The Beggar's Opera was by all odds the most popular theatrical work of the eighteenth century. Its unprecedented first-season run of sixty-two nights (Pope erroneously stated sixty-three) marked it as the first full-fledged hit of the English stage. And it proved to be more than a fad, for it was acted in nearly every year from 1728 to 1886. John Gay's ballad opera—the first of its genre to be produced in England—has left its mark on all subsequent musical comedy, from Gilbert and Sullivan, through *Oklahoma,* down to the present day. So popular was the play in 1728 that decorative screens and fans were manufactured, inscribed with songs from *The Beggar's Opera;* and London was flooded with pictures of the actress who played Polly Peachum. Great actresses have vied for the part of Polly, aware that the role made a duchess of the first Polly and increased the fortunes of many others. Moreover, the phenomenal success of Gay's piece continues unabated. Adapted by Kurt Weill and Bertold Brecht, Gay's rollicking farce has become the long-lived *Three-Penny Opera,* which is still packing in audiences around the world.

Oddly enough, *The Beggar's Opera* almost died at birth, and the world of the theatre very nearly lost one of its most delightful treats. When Gay took his play to Colley Cibber, the shrewd manager of the Drury Lane Theatre, it was flatly refused. Cibber badly misjudged the public taste, but he had logical reasons. After all, in an age thoroughly addicted to Italian opera, how could one make money producing a ballad opera, made up of common street songs and having the avowed purpose of laughing Italian opera off the boards? Also, why should a canny theatrical manager place himself in the vulnerable position of producing such an obvious satire, directed at Court life and at the King's chief minister, Walpole, in particular? Then there was the moral issue, which, as Cibber rightly foresaw, was to be preached about in countless English pulpits and debated endlessly in pamphlets. Gay's unorthodox "pastoral" was set, for the most part, in Newgate Prison, and the cast of characters was made up of the motliest collection of jades, strumpets, bawds, cutpurses, and highwaymen ever assembled on the English stage.

After Cibber's refusal, Gay prevailed upon the Duchess of Queensberry, one of his staunchest supporters, to use her influence to persuade John Rich, manager of the Lincoln's Inn Fields, to give the ballad opera a hearing. Rich was unimpressed, but after the Duchess generously offered to underwrite any losses, he agreed to go ahead with the production. But there were still more pitfalls to come. After the first rehearsal Rich was ready to give up the project, but some of the leading literary men of the century urged him to continue, and he brought out the production at the smallest possible cost. The manager of Lincoln's Inn Fields must have been born under a lucky star. The immediate success of *The Beggar's Opera* led the wags of the day to remark that it made *"Rich* very *Gay,* and will probably make *Gay* very *Rich."*

Gay and his friends Pope and Swift were apprehensive about the success of *The Beggar's Opera,* seemingly more concerned about the public reaction to the new ballad opera form than the reaction to the sharpness of the satire. Pope's account of the opening night's performance on January 29, 1728, conveys vividly the tension that was felt by Gay's friends: "We were all at the first night of it, in great uncertainty of the event; till we were very much encouraged by overhearing the Duke of Argyle, who sat in the box next to us, say, 'it will do,—it must do!—I see it in the eyes of them.'—This was a good while before the first act was over, and so gave us ease soon; for the duke, (besides his own good taste) has a more particular knack than any one now living, in discovering the taste of the public. He was quite right in this, as usual; the good nature of the audience appeared stronger and stronger with every act, and ended in a clamour of applause."

The newspaper reviews following the opening were scanty, but laudatory. The *Daily Journal,* in reporting on "Mr. Gay's new English Opera, written in a manner wholly new, and very entertaining," stated that "no Theatrical Performance for these many Years has met with so much Applause." A weekly newspaper, *The Craftsman,* noted that *The Beggar's Opera* "has met with a general Applause." On February 15 Gay, still unaware how big a theatrical bonanza he had on his hands, wrote to Swift that the opera was acted "with such success, that the playhouse hath been crowded every night. Tonight is the fifteenth time of acting, and it is thought it will run a fortnight longer." In that day of short runs in the theatre, Gay was unable to conceive, in his most optimistic dreams, of his work's attaining a record of sixty-two performances in the first season.

What is the secret of the enormous success of *The Beggar's Opera?* First of all, though each generation has continued to label the piece good theatre and rollicking, high-spirited entertainment, each generation has also had its own special reasons for enjoying Gay's comedy. In the early part of the eighteenth century, before the appearance of *The Beggar's Opera,* the musical taste of the ordinary theatre-goer was virtually ignored. The Italian opera held full sway, despite such satiric comments as Addison's in the *Spectator:* "Our great-grandchildren will be very curious to know the reason why their forefathers used to sit together like an audience of foreigners in their own country, and to hear whole plays acted before them in a tongue they did not understand." The practical man in the street wanted none of this Italianate "squalling," and when *The Beggar's Opera* appeared with its sweet, simple, singable airs—most of them familiar—a popular response was virtually assured. Gay was particularly well qualified to choose ballad airs and to adapt them to his opera. He was an excellent flutist, had a long-standing interest in popular songs, and had already made a name for himself with two songs: "Black-eyed Susan" and " 'Twas When the Seas Were Roaring." The songs of *The Beggar's Opera* continued to be widely sung in the late nineteenth century, and scarcely a Victorian drawing room was without its music sheets of the popular "Cease Your Funning." It was the music in *The Beggar's Opera* that appealed to the Victorian novelist Thackeray, who found in it "a peculiar, hinted, pathetic sweetness and melody. It charms and melts you."

But the popularity of *The Beggar's Opera* lies deeper than its music. Gay's work spoke out in bold tones against class distinction, the Court, and the King's minister, Walpole. Gay broke from the genteel tradition of Restoration comedy and dared to rebel—as no English playwright for thirty-five years had dared to do —against the shocking inequalities of the society of his day. Gay used a clever method of scrutinizing class relationships: he simply inverted the classes. Within the framework of the opera, the beggars, strumpets, and cutpurses are presented as being of more consequence than the peers who govern the nation. The thieves and whores, in burlesquing the manners of fine lords and ladies, made Gay's point that human nature is the same the world over. It would be difficult for a reader in the twentieth century to understand how fresh a notion this was in the eighteenth century.

In *The Beggar's Opera* the joke was on gamesters, lawyers, courtiers, and politicians—in short, on every-one who made his way at the expense of society. More specifically, the joke was on Walpole, who is variously imaged in the roles of Macheath, Mr. Peachum, and Robin of Bagshot. In the underworld in which this trio moves, peculation, bribery, and treachery form a way of life. Gay suggested that Walpole's government thrived by the same methods. Sir Robert Walpole, it

should be noted, took the satire amiably enough. A
contemporary account tells of Walpole's attending the
opening night of the opera. The audience demanded an
encore of the song sung by Lockit,

> When you censure the age,
> Be cautious and sage,
> Lest the courtiers offended should be.
> If you mention vice or bribe,
> 'Tis so pat to all the tribe
> Each cries—That was leveled at me.

All eyes turned to Walpole as the song was being sung,
and Sir Robert noted how pointedly the audience applied the lines to him. At the end of the encore, Walpole
repeated, in a loud voice, the last line: "That was
leveled at me!" This so delighted the audience that it
blunted Gay's barb and earned the prime minister
general applause.

In regard to specific social issues, Gay sends some
sharp satiric darts at the corrupt prison system of that
day. In Act II Macheath is able to get a lighter, more
comfortable set of irons by offering the jailor a bribe.
Later, a bribe enables him to escape from Newgate.
By implication, Gay is striking out at a system that
exacted capital punishment for petty thievery and allowed such parasites as Peachum to make a good living
by turning informant.

Another popular aspect of *The Beggar's Opera* was
its literary burlesque. Early eighteenth-century audiences were well grounded in literature—current and
classical—and came to the theatre prepared to laugh
at such intellectual subtleties as the spoofing of literary
and dramatic forms. The audience had plenty of such
subtleties to cogitate upon in *The Beggar's Opera,*
which has been called by one early editor of the work
the finest burlesque in the English language. Gay's
basic technique was to present, simply and solemnly,
a band of crooks and molls that were the very antithesis
of the casts then prevalent in sentimental comedies by

Cibber and Steele. The sentimental comedy of the day
had gone to ludicrous excesses of artificiality and
bathos; thus when the highwayman Macheath ex-
changes soft and tender dialogues with his two tarts
in Act I, the audience found the parody of contemporary
comedy delicious. Polly's soliloquy in scene xii, Act I,
is a prime example of Gay's ability to turn sentimentality
into a jest. Note the extravagance of her words as she
contemplates the demise of her highwayman-lover:

> Now I'm a wretch, indeed—methinks I see him
> already in the cart, sweeter and more lovely
> than the nosegay in his hand!—I hear the crowd
> extolling his resolution and intrepidity!—What
> volleys of sighs are sent from the windows of Holborn,
> that so comely a youth should be brought to disgrace!
> —I see him at the tree! The whole circle are in tears!
> —even butchers weep!

Comedy which depends upon the burlesque of another
literary or dramatic form is rare in our time. The
technique is sometimes used in musical comedies, a
notable example being a satire on English musical
comedies of the 1920's, "The Boy Friend," a perennial
favorite in off-Broadway theatres and on the straw-hat
circuit. Also, Sid Caesar's television comedy often
takes the form of burlesquing early silent movies and
sentimental comedies of the gas-light era.

Certainly another reason for the popularity of *The
Beggar's Opera* was the great interest of Londoners
in crime and the characters of the underworld. This
interest had been stimulated in 1725 by an incident
involving two of the most notorious criminals of the
time, Jonathan Wild and Joseph Blake. Wild, who was
then public enemy number one, was a receiver of
stolen goods and may have been the prototype of
Peachum in *The Beggar's Opera*. Wild instigated the
arrest of Blake, and at the trial in Old Bailey, Blake
attacked his betrayer with a penknife, almost killing
him. This attack at the trial captured the imagination
of all London and prompted pamphlets, engraved

prints, and ballads to be prepared and sold on the subject. Gay wrote a ballad called *Newgate's Garland: Being a New Ballad, Shewing How Mr. Jonathan Wild's Throat was cut from Ear to Ear with a penknife, by Mr. Blake, alias Blueskin, the bold Highwayman, as he stood his Tryal in the Old-Bailey*. Jonathan Wild lived to betray another highwayman, Jack Sheppard, before being hanged himself in May of 1725. These underworld characters left their mark upon the English stage. In 1725 the play *The Prison Break, or the Adventures of Jack Sheppard* appeared. In 1727 Christopher Bullock's prison play, *Match in Newgate* was performed. All this set the stage for *The Beggar's Opera*, a work which is infinitely superior to anything of its type that had preceded it.

Another factor in the early popularity of *The Beggar's Opera* was the noisy controversy regarding the morality of the play. Although the general public accepted the piece as the good-natured farce it was, some moralists of the day saw it as an instructor of vice and perdition. This reaction came early. In March, 1728, the Rev. Thomas Herring, a court chaplain and preacher at Lincoln's Inn Chapel denounced the criminal influence of Gay's work in a sermon that was widely quoted. *Mist's Weekly Journal* of March 30, 1728, stated that Herring "inveighed against it, as a Thing of every evil Tendency." Gay took the assault lightly, writing to Swift: "I suppose you must have heard, that I had the Honour to have had a sermon preached against my works by a Court Chaplain, which I look upon as no small Addition to my Fame." But many took the matter seriously. William Duncombe, an editor of Dr. Herring's sermons, stated, in regard to the attack on *The Beggar's Opera*: "He was not singular in this Opinion; and Experience afterwards confirmed the Truth of his Observations, since several Thieves and Street-robbers confessed in *Newgate,* that they raised their Courage at the Playhouse, by the Songs of their Hero *Macheath,* before they sallied forth on their desperate nocturnal Exploits." It was Jonathan Swift, himself a clergyman in the Anglican Church, who came to Gay's defense after Dr. Herring's attack. Swift gave a strong voice to the idea that Gay's work had "placed Vice of all kinds in the strongest and most odious light; and thereby done eminent service both to Religion and Morality." He added, in reference to Dr. Herring's outcry, that *The Beggar's Opera* "will probably do more good than a thousand bad sermons."

But Swift's defense did not silence the outcry that Gay's play was corrupting the nation's morals. *Mist's Weekly Journal,* seeming to question the motives of those opposing Gay's play, reported that "certain People, of an envious disposition, attribute the Frequency of the late Robberies to the success of the Beggar's Opera, and the Pleasure the Town takes in the Character and Impunity of Captain Macheath." A letter in the *London Journal* conjectured as to how much Gay's comedy "may have contributed (contrary to the Intention of the Author) towards those daring Attacks which are daily committed on the Property of the Subject in the Streets of our Capital." Daniel Defoe, who was as strait-laced a moralist as any, condemned the play in *Augusta Triumphans* (1728): "We take great pains to puff 'em up in their villainy, and thieves are set out in so amiable a light in 'The Beggar's Opera' that it has taught them to value themselves on their profession, rather than be asham'd of it by making a highwayman the hero and dismissing him at last unpunished." The drama was prohibited in France in 1750 because the cast was composed of underworld characters and also because of the moral implications of the hero's escaping punishment. In 1773 an attempt was made to force the actor-producer Garrick from presenting the opera on the grounds that it "never was represented on the stage without creating an additional number of real thieves." The morality question has continued to plague producers of *The Beggar's Opera* throughout its history. Today, however, the question is almost academic. The truth of the matter is that Gay's play mirrored a corrupt and coarse age, and it mirrored it with the realism of a Hogarth.

There is no doubt that *The Beggar's Opera* is good theatre—its popularity through the centuries is proof enough of that. But is it a good play? An analysis of the construction of Gay's comedy, its characterizations, and its plot will give the answer.

When analyzing the structure of *The Beggar's Opera,* the modern reader will note first of all that the play is cut up into an unusually large number of scenes. The first act has thirteen scenes, the second fifteen, and the third seventeen. Forty-five changes of scene, then, split the play into fragments, with some of the scenes comprising only a few lines of soliloquy and others developing the action extensively with a stage full of players. Such a kaleidoscope of changes is not suitable to modern tastes. Even in the nineteenth century a two-act version was written to overcome some of the technical problems of production and to give the play a tighter and more unified construction. But a deeper analysis of the structure shows that Gay knew what he was doing. The quick changes of scenery—more in keeping with the art of the motion picture than the stage—gave Gay precisely the hard-driving, brisk movement he wanted. The action never lags, and the audience is compelled along by the rhythmic stresses of one scene being contrasted with another.

To keep the forty-five scenes from becoming a maze to confound his audience, Gay used a simple thread of action to tie his incidents together. This was also a part of his method of satirizing the bombastic extravagances of Italian opera and heroic tragedy. Also, Gay looks ahead to the techniques of modern comedy by beginning most of the scenes *in medias res*—in the middle of the action. Gay likewise was able to contrive dramatic climax and theatrical surprise with his choppy construction, for he was able to use his superb sense of timing to an advantage. Macheath's entrances in the first two acts are good examples of Gay's skill in this regard. The tavern scene in which Macheath is betrayed by his libertine ladies is an illustration of Gay's ability to build to a dramatic climax. All in all, despite the multiplicity of scenes, there is an organic unity in the play, with one scene leading naturally to another.

Any discussion of the merits of *The Beggar's Opera* must focus on the characterization. It was here that Gay was most original, for he brought to the English stage a cast unlike any then being seen on the boards. Remarkably, despite the bizarre character of his players, Gay manages to make them real people rather than caricatures. Generally speaking, all are humorous characters, with many of the names—like Peachum, Lockit, Filch, and Trapes—suggesting the occupation of their owners. Interestingly enough, if one leaves out the Beggar, the Player, and the chorus, there are exactly twelve men and twelve women, neatly poised like two teams in the battle of the sexes. From this group six important roles emerge: Macheath, his two loves—Polly and Lucy, Mr. and Mrs. Peachum, and Lockit. Two minor characters, Filch and Diana Trapes, have a small relation to the plot as individuals, but the remainder of the minor roles enter into the action only collectively.

Although the role of Polly Peachum has long been given the lion's share of popularity, there is no doubt that much of the action and the humor of the play revolves around the character of Macheath. He is the romantic, suave gentleman-highwayman, the darling of all the trollops of Hockley-in-the-Hole, Vinegar Yard, and Lewkner's Lane. This seamy gallant woos and wins Polly and Lucy, and at the rousing finish of the play he is claimed by "four wives more." Macheath, the dashing knight of the highway after dark and the lover and gamester by day, is respected by common robbers as well as by the gentlemen gamblers whom he generously accommodates at the tables at Marybone. Something in his manner suggests that he might indeed be the scapegrace son of nobility who prefers his own free life to that of the restricted aristocracy. He dresses like a dandy and speaks the King's English; yet he is at home among his own, faithful always to his cutthroat friends. He is a paradox: he is chivalrous, gay, polite; he is an accomplished highwayman who is courteous to those he robs and who eschews violence and brutality. William Hazlitt, the literary critic, gave his opinions about how the role should be played after seeing a performance of the play in 1816: "His gallantry and good-breeding should arise from impulse, not from rule; not from the trammels of education, but from a soul generous, courageous, good-natured, aspiring, amorous. The class of the character is difficult to hit. It is something between gusto and slang, like portwine and brandy mixed. It is not the mere gentleman that should be represented, but the blackguard sublimated into the gentleman."

Polly Peachum's role has won the hearts of all of Gay's audiences, and rightfully so. She is the sweet, simple, trusting foil to all the remainder of the underworld entourage. She is the wide-eyed ingénue who adores Macheath and can never see his falseness. Even though Macheath deceives Polly, the audience can still believe he loves her, for who could not love so dainty and artless a lass? It is said that in the opening performance of the play when Polly knelt before her father and mother and pleaded for the life of her lover with a sweet, plaintive ballad, the success of the production was assured. One can well imagine the audience's acceptance of the song, sung to the old ballad air, "The Children in the Wood":

> On ponder well! be not severe;
>   So save a wretched wife!
> For on the rope that hangs my dear
>   Depends poor Polly's life.

Lucy Lockit, the remaining third of Gay's love triangle, is the very antithesis of Polly. In fits of anger she can be as coarse as any inmate of Newgate Prison, where she lives with her father, the jailor. She does not find it easy to forgive Macheath's trifling with her affections. She is jealous and vengeful, even to the extent of a plot to poison Polly. With it all, she is simple enough for Macheath to deceive with the flimsiest of explanations. Near the end of the play the audience is likely to find that despite her flaws she has come to be a thoroughly likeable character.

Peachum, although he is one of the most despicable characters in the play, has such a philosophical and humorous bent to his view of life that his evil is tempered and mitigated. He lives off the criminal world as a "fence," or receiver of stolen goods, and when the fancy strikes him, he informs on his clients to receive the standard forty-pound reward. Incidentally, few of those he informed on were able to avenge themselves, for hanging was the punishment in the early eighteenth century for even so petty a crime as the theft of a handkerchief. An example of Peachum's offbeat philosophy of life is found in the opening lines of the play: "A lawyer is an honest employment; so is mine. Like me, too, he acts in a double capacity, both against rogues and for 'em; for 'tis but fitting that we should protect and encourage cheats, since we live by 'em." A few lines later he says, "I love to let women 'scape. A good sportsman always lets the hen partridges fly, because the breed of the game depends upon them." From such statements as these one gets the impression of Peachum's roguish individuality. He is a student of human nature who has promoted his studies into a comfortable living at the expense of the most expendable class of society.

Mrs. Peachum, who appears only in the first act, also has an inverted view of society and a way with a witty phrase. When she learns that Macheath, her prospective son-in-law, has been consorting with the gentry, she is alarmed. "What business hath he to keep company with lords and gentlemen?" she queries; "he should leave them to prey upon one another." Her rather bizarre notions about matrimony are shown in Act I, as she soliloquizes over the possibility of Polly's marriage: "Why must our Polly, forsooth, differ from her sex, and love only her husband? And why must Polly's marriage, contrary to all observation, make her less followed by other men? All men are thieves in love, and like a woman the better for being another's property."

Lockit, who is the turnkey at Newgate Prison, is on one level the typical *petit bourgeois* officeholder, proud of the power his position brings. On the other hand, he is shrewd enough to work with Peachum on his unscrupulous deals and indeed is as evil as his partner, but he lacks Peachum's wit. Although he does not appear until the second act, he is important in the development of the plot.

Of the remaining minor characters, it is Filch, the young rascal who plies his art of picking pockets with all the professional pride of a surgeon, who stands out. Mrs. Peachum says of him: "He hath as fine a hand at picking a pocket as has a woman, and is as nimble-fingered as a juggler." Filch was a great favorite with the pit, for he was assigned one of the bawdiest bits of humor in the play. In Act III Filch is in Newgate "helping the ladies to a pregnancy against their being called down to sentence." His next line always sent the rabble into choruses of raucous laughter: "But if a man cannot get an honest livelihood any easier way, I am sure 'tis what I can't undertake for another session."

The remaining characters, in terms of the action of the play, are best thought of collectively. One of the most ingenious creations in the play is the gang of highwaymen, with their descriptive names: Jemmy Twitcher, Crook-fingered Jack, Wat Dreary, Robin of Bagshot, Nimming Ned, Harry Padington, Matt of the Mint, and Ben Budge. This band of rogues, speaking of themselves as a "set of practical philosophers," provides much of the satire of the play as they open the second act with the famous tavern scene. Gay uses these gangsters to satirize the morals of courtiers in particular. For example:

> NED: Who is there here that would not die for his friend?
>
> HARRY: Who is there here that would betray him for his interest?
>
> MATT: Show me a gang of courtiers who can say as much.

Macheath's gang also has much to say about one of the chief objects of Gay's satire: improper attitudes toward money. William Empson has pointed out that every reference to money in *The Beggar's Opera* contains some satire on the normal attitudes toward it. Sven M. Armens, in his book, *John Gay, Social Critic,* states that "Gay's great objection in both his poetry and dramas is that money is being constantly misused and overesteemed." In the passages about money Gay is not satirizing the aristocracy so much as he is the rising bourgeoisie, the Whig mercantile class, that was rapidly gaining power through the control of shops and manufacturing processes. Gay felt that the love of the middle class for money led to hypocrisy and greed. He attacks this through a speech by Matt of the Mint, who says, "The world is avaricious, and I hate avarice. A covetous fellow, like a jackdaw, steals what he was never made to enjoy, for the sake of hiding it. These are the robbers of mankind, for money was made for the free-hearted and generous."

Comparable to the eight highwayman are eight women of the London demimonde whom Gay uses to satirize the ladies of high society in the fourth scene of Act II. Here Gay pokes fun at the ladies of gentility by having his trulls imitate them in dress, manners, and conversational topics. And again the names are monuments to Gay's ingenious wit: Mrs. Coaxer, Dolly Trull, Mrs. Vixen, Betty Doxy, Jenny Diver, Mrs. Slammekin, Suky Tawdry, and Molly Brazen. The famous scene featuring Macheath and his eight ladies is memorable for many witticisms that would do credit to an Oscar Wilde or a George Bernard Shaw. Molly Brazen's aphorism is typical: "To cheat a man is nothing; but the woman must have fine parts indeed who cheats a woman."

The marvel of Gay's characterizations is that despite the grotesque nature of his players, despite their unusual names, and despite the inversion of the expected manners and speech patterns, there is an air of realism about them. One feels that Gay has an intimate knowledge of the London life he presents. A. P. Herbert, the author of *Mr. Gay's London,* has studied the "Proceedings of London Sessions from December, 1732, to October, 1733." The court trials prove that Gay was in no way exaggerating the situation. Mr. Herbert remarks that "realizing for the first time the material he had at hand, one gives him new credit for understatement and artistic restraint." Although Gay's fictional names are cleverly derived, he had much bizarre raw material to work with. Some of the actual names recorded in the sessional proceedings are Barbara Dewfly, Matthew Monger, Susan Marriage, and Robert Bugbeard. Other historians of the period have commented on the high incidence of crime in the early eighteenth century, with its ridiculous standards for imposing the death penalty. Persons were hanged for stealing 40 shillings from a dwelling house, five shillings from a shop, or 12½ pence from a pocket. Murder and arson, however, were classed as misdemeanors, and Gay was close to the truth when he had Peachum comment: "Murder is as fashionable a crime as a man can be guilty of." Despite the liberties Gay has taken in order to promote his satire, the atmosphere is undeniably authentic.

The plot of *The Beggar's Opera,* when stripped of nonessentials, is a very simple narrative, ideally suited as a vehicle for Gay's satire and wit. The play opens with a prologue, in the form of a dialogue between a Player and the Beggar, who is posing as the author. In the prologue Gay gets in many of his gibes at Italian opera. He says, "I have introduced the similes that are in your celebrated operas: the Swallow, the Moth, the Bee, the Ship, the Flower, etc." He also makes an allusion to a well-known quarrel between two popular opera singers of the day, Faustina and Cuzzoni. These two divas had an argument over who was to have the leading part in an opera during the 1727 season, and all London took sides. Faustina had been imported in 1726 at a salary of 2,500 pounds, while Cuzzoni, already established, received only 2,000 pounds. Cuzzoni, despite what the music authority Burney called her "native warble" and "perfect shake," was dumpy and rather unattractive; Faustina, possessed of a voice that was called "miraculous" in that day, was stunning to behold. It can be assumed that the argument between Polly and Lucy was understood by the audience to refer to the Faustina-Cuzzoni controversy.

In the first scene of the play, Peachum, seated with his account book, sings of his confirmed belief in the dishonesty of everyone, setting the tone of the play immediately. The principal action of the first act concerns the alarm the Peachums feel over the possibility of Polly's marriage to Macheath. It should be noted that the Peachums's objection to the marriage is purely for business reasons. Polly is needed because, as Peachum says, "A handsome wench in our way of business is as profitable as at the bar of a Temple coffee-house." Also, it is feared that Macheath, after becoming a part of the family, will learn too many of Peachum's secrets. After questioning Filch, however, Mrs. Peachum discovers that Polly is already married to Macheath. After much discussion the parents agree that the only action possible now is to inform on their son-in-law and keep the reward in the family. Polly pleads for her lover's life, but the Peachums are adamant. She goes to tell Macheath of the danger, concluding the first act.

Act II opens with Macheath's gang assembled in a tavern near Newgate. Macheath enters and explains to the gang that he has had a "slight difference" with Peachum. When his cutthroat cohorts want to do Peachum in, Macheath explains that Peachum is a "necessary agent" and that "Business cannot go on without him." Macheath hopes to make Peachum believe that he has left the gang. The highwayman then assembles eight ladies of the town for a party, but the demireps show their gratitude by secretly disarming him as they embrace him, then signalling for Peachum and the Constable. Macheath is arrested and led away while the ladies argue as to how the reward will be divided. At Newgate the imprisoned captain is given a choice of light or heavy sets of irons by Lockit, the jailor. A handsome bribe persuades Lockit to give Macheath a light set that "will fit as easy as a glove." Macheath is not entirely comfortable in Newgate, however, for he must face Lucy, the outraged and jealous daughter of the jailor. He deceives her by denying his marriage to Polly and succeeds in calming Lucy by promising her marriage. Later Lucy agrees to arrange an escape for Macheath, but the ill-timed arrival of Polly, crying: "Where is my dear husband?" almost thwarts this plan. The easily gulled Lucy is again deceived by Macheath, however, and the escape is made at the close of Act II.

At the beginning of Act III, Lockit discovers that his daughter has allowed Macheath to escape. Peachum and Lockit learn the whereabouts of the captain from Mrs. Diana Trapes and go to apprehend him. Meanwhile, Lucy attempts to get revenge by offering Polly a glass of poisoned wine. Professor Frederick S. Boas finds this attempt to poison Polly the only feature of the play that seems out of key. Polly, suspicious of the potion, drops the glass as she sees Macheath brought into custody. The two daughters then kneel before their respective fathers to plead for their lover's life. This scene, always a favorite, is the subject of a Hogarth painting. The fathers are obdurate, and Macheath is led away to be tried at Old Bailey. The next scene

finds Macheath in the condemned hold, drinking wine.
He also sings Gay's parody of the operatic recitativo;
Macheath sings a medley, linking phrases out of nine
familiar tunes and swigging from a bottle after nearly
every phrase. Two members of the gang come in to
pay their condolences, and Macheath makes them vow
to see Peachum and Lockit hanged for their villainy.
Polly and Lucy come in, and Macheath advises them
to go to the West Indies and find a "husband apiece."
At this moment a jailor announces that there are four
more of Macheath's wives seeking to gain audience
with him, and the highwayman calls for the hangman
out of sheer desperation. The Beggar and the Player
enter at this point, with the Player arguing that
Macheath should not be executed. The Beggar answers
that in order for the play to satisfy poetic justice, the
highwayman must be hanged. The Player argues that
this makes it a "downright deep tragedy" and adds that
"an opera must end happily." The Beggar decides to
rectify the ending, and he sends one of the rabble in to
inform Macheath of his reprieve. This part of the play is
nothing more than satire directed against Italian opera;
the Player comments, "All this we must do to comply
with the taste of the town." Macheath and the others
come on stage again, and the highwayman confesses
that he is legally married to Polly. The play concludes
with a riotous dance.

It is evident that the plot is scanty, but it is diverting
and of sufficient stature to provide a framework for the
fun-making, and nothing more is needed. Perhaps one
should not look for a moral in such a tale, for it is
evident that Gay was more intent on presenting a good
show than in raising moral standards. However, we
need not overlook the implications of the Beggar's long
speech at the end. Coming, as it does, immediately
following the light-hearted reprieve of Macheath, it
might easily be taken less seriously than Gay intended
it. It does give an opportunity for Gay, speaking
through the guise of the Beggar, to comment on and
summarize the play. The Beggar says:

Through the whole piece you may observe such a similitude of manners in high and low life, that it is difficult to determine whether (in the fashionable vices) the fine gentlemen imitate the gentlemen of the road, or the gentlemen of the road the fine gentlemen. Had the play remained as I at first intended, it would have carried a most excellent moral. 'Twould have shown that the lower sort of people have their vices in a degree as well as the rich, and that they are punished for them.

There is no doubt that an eighteenth-century audience—provided they were able to stop laughing long enough to think—would have found much to discuss in this bold and liberal statement of what amounts to a social philosophy. As John C. Loftis states in this book, *Comedy and Society from Congreve to Fielding,* "We should be more inclined to see bold social comment in *The Beggar's Opera* had the subsequent history of England produced a revolution." Even if the Beggar's ironic quip about the iron-bound classes in English society were overlooked, no one in the audience should have missed Ben Budge's revolutionary remark: "We are for a just partition of the world, for every man has a right to enjoy life."

Some understanding of Gay's intent in writing *The Beggar's Opera* can be gained from tracing the work from its genesis to its final form. Very likely the idea for the work was planted in Gay's mind by Jonathan Swift. Swift wrote to Pope on August 30, 1716, about an ingenious young Quaker in the town who wrote verses to his mistress. This suggested to Swift that "a set of Quaker pastorals might succeed, if our friend Gay could fancy it." It was the final sentence of the paragraph, however, that was to bear fruit. "Or what think you," he asked, "of a Newgate pastoral, among the thieves and whores there?" Pope tells us of Gay's reaction to Swift's immodest proposal: "Gay was inclined to try such a thing, for some time, but afterwards thought it would be better to write a comedy on the same plan. This was what gave rise to the Beggar's Opera." It is fortunate that Gay chose to cast the idea in the form of a comedy rather than a pastoral. It is also fortunate that Gay chose to postpone the writing of the opera from 1716 to 1727. At the later date Gay was as ready for the task as London was ready to receive it. His intimate acquaintance with the low types who were to people his play as well as with the songs they were to sing made his preparation complete. Also, the events of the intervening years were to whet the public's appetite for stories of the underworld, and the vogue for Italian opera had reached such absurd heights that it was ripe to be satirized. He wrote the play at Pope's estate at Twickenham in 1727, amid congenial surroundings that must have added to the mood of merriment that produced the opera.

At first no one quite knew how to take Gay's neither-fish-nor-fowl theatrical work. Congreve, after reading the manuscript, said that it would "either take greatly, or be damned confoundly." History has proved Congreve's prediction to be partly a shrewd one, for the opera "took" greatly. And the fact of this success, along with the facts of the genesis of the work from Swift's suggestion, must be considered in an attempted evaluation of Gay's intent in writing the play. Obviously, the talented, but as yet unsuccessful, man of letters was intent on giving the public what he thought it wanted. In this period of his life, full of frustration as he attempted to win favor at the court, he yearned for success—and success he won in a generous measure. It is a tribute to Gay's genius that in the process of engineering a hit, he incidentally pioneered in a new musical comedy form, laughed the Italian opera off the boards, restored comedy to its once-high status, and delivered bold satiric thrusts at society, the prison system, the court, and the prime minister. But as to Gay's moral intent, one finally must agree with Samuel Johnson that *The Beggar's Opera* was "written to divert, without any moral purpose."

So akin are the dialogue and the songs in *The Beggar's Opera* that one cannot be considered without the other, and there is no doubt that the music contributed greatly to the success of the play. Gay was well aware of the growing popularity of popular songs and ballads in his day. At this time Thomas Cross, a music engraver, was printing and selling great numbers of songs on half sheets. Gay, himself an accomplished flutist as well as a lover of street balladry, was just the person to translate the growing public interest in songs into a work for the theatre. Thus the sixty-nine songs which he wrote to a variety of popular tunes became a highly original contribution to the theatre. Gay chose sundry English and Scotch tunes, ranging from zesty, jig-like dances to dignified, hymn-like airs. Most of the tunes are old and familiar ballad and dance airs, but there are a few contemporary popular songs. It is remarkable that Gay, in putting his words to the familiar music, put his permanent mark on the tunes as well. Many of the tunes, though quite old in 1728, are now thought of as *Beggar's Opera* airs. And, despite the disparity and variety of the tunes—some sad, some joyous—Gay has somehow managed to make them homogeneous. The homogeneity comes from the atmosphere of the melodies, for Gay's tunes all evoke the eighteenth century, with its songbooks, ballad singers, coffeehouses, and taverns. As James Boswell puts it, "I know from my own experience, that Scotch reels, though brisk, make me melancholy . . . whereas the airs in 'The Beggar's Opera,' many of which are very soft, never fail to render me gay, because they are associated with the warm sensations and high spirits of London."

Gay got his musical suggestions from several collections of songs, including Thomas D'Urfey's *Wit and Mirth, or Pills to Purge Melancholy* (6 vols., 1719–20) and William Thomson's *Orpheus Caledonius* (a folio volume, 1726). But Gay entirely rewrote the original songs to suit his opera. A few examples, comparing the originals to *The Beggar's Opera* adaptations, will show the brilliance of Gay's versions. Many of Gay's songs bear almost no resemblance to the original. The first song in the opera is a biting satirical thrust:

> Through all the employments of life,
>   Each neighbor abuses his brother;
> Whore and rogue they call husband and wife:
>   All professions be-rogue one another.
> The priest calls the lawyer a cheat,
>   The lawyer be-knaves the divine;
> And the statesman, because he's so great,
>   Thinks his trade as honest as mine.

This is quite a distance artistically from the popular ballad from which the tune comes:

> An old Woman Cloathed in Grey,
> Whose Daughter was charming and young,
> But Chanc'd to be once led astray,
> By Roger's false flattering Tongue.
> With whom she too often had been,
> Abroad in the meadows and Field.

In scene viii of Act I Gay has Polly sing her tearful song in defense of her love:

> Can love be controlled by advice?
>   Will Cupid our mothers obey?
> Though my heart were as frozen as ice,
>   At his flame 'twould have melted away.
>
> When he kissed me, so closely he pressed,
>   'Twas so sweet that I must have complied,
> So I thought it both safest and best
>   To marry, for fear you should chide.

This bears no similarity to the original, which comes from the *Roxburghe Ballads* and bears the early title: "The Lunatick Lover: or, The Young Man's Call to Grim King of the Ghosts for Cure":

> Grim King of the Ghosts, make hast,
> And bring hither all your train;

See how the Pale Moon do's wast!
    And just now is in the Wain:

Come you Night-Hags, with your Charms,
And revelling Witches away,
And hug me close in your Arms,
    To you my Respects I'll pay.

Possibly because the ballad opera was a new and untried theatrical form in England, *The Beggar's Opera* was put into production with no thought of having an orchestra accompany the singers. At the "second last rehearsal" Rich, the theatrical manager, suggested that instruments be added. Dr. J. C. Pepusch was then called in to arrange the tunes and to compose an overture. Dr. Pepusch, a scholarly German musician, composed an original overture based on variations of the song, "I'm Like a Skiff." Although the orchestra in the pit was small—consisting of several violins, a hautboy, and a drum—the overture and the incidental music was well received. The music, however, was responsible for a *faux pas* that occurred on the opening night of the play. The audience, unacquainted with the nature of Gay's opera, expected to hear the usual music before the drawing up of the curtain. They felt that they were being cheated out of what was known as the "first and second music," and they began to stamp their feet, scream, and whistle. One Jack Hall was called upon to explain to the audience that it was a rule to have no music prior to the overture. As a contemporary account relates the story: "Jack made his obeisance with tolerable grace, but being confounded at the general silence which so suddenly ensued on his appearance, blundered out—'Ladies and gentlemen, we—we—beg you'll not call for first and second music, because—because you all know, that there is never any music at all in an opera.' This bull put the house in good humour, and the piece proceeded."

And so it was that the world's best-loved musical play was produced. And from that January day in

London in 1728, the opera has continued to lead a
storied life down through the ages. *The Beggar's Opera*
was the first musical play to be produced in colonial
New York. The Murray-Kean Company of London
players applied to Governor Clinton in 1750, hired
a hall on Nassau Street, and produced Gay's comedy.
It was George Washington's favorite entertainment,
and he saw a production of it whenever he could. There
is also evidence that the famous quarrel between
Alexander Hamilton and Aaron Burr was precipitated
by the Polly Peachum of the company then playing
the opera. When the play was revived in London in
1920 at the Lyric Theatre, it ran for 1,463 performances, and in that same year a production opened at
the Greenwich Village Theatre in New York. In 1923
there was a *Beggar's Opera* Club with membership
limited to those who had seen at least forty performances of the opera. There have been several recent
revivals of the play, including John Gielgud's London
production in 1940, the Interplayers' New York production in 1950, and the Cambridge Drama Festival
production (also produced at the New York City
Center) in 1958. Sir Laurence Olivier starred as Captain Macheath in a movie version of the play, and
Duke Ellington wrote the music for a Broadway
musical based on Gay's play and entitled *The Beggar's
Holiday*. Gay's play is one of those rare literary works,
a truly popular classic.

THE STAGING

The theatres of the early part of the eighteenth century were markedly different from those of Shakespeare's day. After the Restoration the playhouses were constructed as closed, indoor theatres, and the old arena form was abandoned. The Restoration theatre, however, still clung to a relic of the old Elizabethan platform stage. Until the end of the seventeenth century the playhouses had wide, deep aprons that extended as far forward from the proscenium arch as the stage proper stretched behind. This allowed the actors to stride forward on the platform and orate their lines near the center of the auditorium. The modifying of this platform stage was one of the most important changes made in this era in the structure of theatres, and it was accomplished by Christopher Rich, father of the John Rich who produced *The Beggar's Opera* at Lincoln's Inn Fields Theatre in 1728.

About 1696 the elder Rich, then the manager of the Drury Lane Theatre, cut off part of the apron stage in order to gain extra room in the theatre. He also removed two of the entrance doors that stood on each side. These front, or lower, doors were converted into stage boxes, and two more doors were built behind the proscenium arch. With the reduced apron, squared at the end, the theatres of the eighteenth century were not greatly different from modern playhouses. The drop curtains and the scene of action were somewhat far removed from the spectators by modern standards, but the actors compensated by walking as far forward as they could on some speeches. The orchestra now had its place in front of the stage and was no longer in a box or gallery above or beside it. The proscenium continued to be very deep and was richly ornamented with gilt pilasters. There were latticed boxes for spectators just above the stage—so close that a lady could, if she desired, pluck the plume from an actor's hat.

In John Gay's time there was a curtain at the proscenium arch, but it was rarely used as it is in the modern theatre. In general the curtain was raised after the prologue and kept open during the performance, not lowered and raised between acts. Scenes were usually changed by closing or opening flat sets. The sets were designed in an ingenious manner, with all the pieces of a setting supported in horizontal grooves. The sets could easily be slid into place, and it is interesting that all of the opening and closing of scenery by sliding took place before the eyes of the audience. Indeed, this was a part of the excitement and spectacle of a swiftly moving show. The system of visible scene-changing was so firmly a part of the British theatrical tradition that the actors would often remain on stage when the occasion demanded no more than their moving from one place to another. Instead of the actors leaving the stage, the scene itself slid away and another replaced it, with the players going ahead with the action.

The audience sat in a fan-shaped auditorium which had a pit, middle and upper galleries, and boxes. The pit, with its uncomfortable benches, was considered in the early part of the century to be no place for a gentleman. Here the lower classes laughed uproariously and fought among themselves if the play became boring. Since the deeper plays were frequently boring to the occupants of the pit, fights were numerous; and when the passions became inflamed the auditorium would look like a battlefield, with the combatants having at each other with chairs, benches, and swords. Later in the century the pit became more fashionable and was thought to contain the most discriminating part of the audience. The bottom row of boxes was long considered to be the most fashionable, however, with the middle gallery (or pit balcony) being less *comme il faut*. The middle gallery contained the genteel courtesans as well as the middle-class citizens. The upper gallery was the haunt of the servants and the unruly rabble. In the latter half of the seventeenth century it was the custom to allow lackeys free admission during the last act of a play. The pouring in of these late arrivals always created a great disturbance and was a nuisance to the actors. At the turn of the century a small fee called "after-money" was collected, somewhat alleviating the situation, but it did not long deter the tradition that the rabble in the upper galleries were to be as noisy and rambunctious as they were able to be. In 1732, after the pit became more fashionable, a ticket to the pit or the lowest boxes cost five shillings, the middle gallery two shillings, and the high gallery one shilling. The prices were raised considerably on first nights and for special performances, and on these nights the proceeds might run as high as £500 or £600. This is remarkable when one considers that some of the theatres were quite small; John Rich's Covent Garden Theatre, opened in 1732, was 51 feet from the stage to the back of the boxes. Rich ecomomized on space by allowing only 21 inches per person.

The Beggar's Opera was first produced on January 29, 1728, at John Rich's theatre at Lincoln's Inn Fields. This theatre and the Drury Lane were the privileged houses in the first part of the century. It was Christopher Rich, John's father, who had begun the rebuilding of Lincoln's Inn Fields Theatre, but he died six weeks before the project was completed. John Rich opened the playhouse on December 8 (other sources say November 18), 1714. According to contemporary reports, the theatre was a handsome building, with the interior superbly adorned with mirrors on each side. The stage was furnished with new scenery which was the envy of the rival playhouse. Although *The Beggar's Opera* had its first production in the Lincoln's Inn Fields Theatre, the ballad opera had a longer association with the Covent Garden Theatre, which Rich erected in 1732 largely with the proceeds from Gay's smashingly successful comedy. This theatre was one of the most magnificent ever seen in London. Rich com-

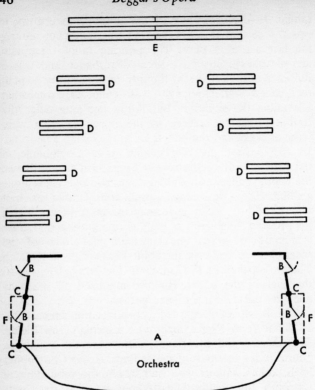

Sketch-Plan of the Covent Garden Theatre, 1732

Although the play was originally presented at the Lincoln's Inn Fields Theatre, it had a longer association with the better-known Covent Garden, which is sketched above. *A* is the fore-stage, beneath the proscenium arch, where most of the action took place. *B* indicates the doors; the front, or lower, doors were beneath the proscenium arch. *C* indicates the main posts supporting the proscenium arch. The wings are indicated by *D*, and the rear shutters by *E*. The dotted lines at the letter *F* indicate the latticed stage boxes which ran onto the stage above the proscenium doors.

missioned the Italian artist Amiconi to do the decorations, and the beautiful ceiling, representing the gods banqueting in the clouds, was the talk of the town. Amiconi also did the scenery with the assistance of an English artist, George Lambert. The theatre was designed with a heavy and elaborate column-treatment of the stage boxes and the whole proscenium unit. There were two "doors of entrance," a legacy from Elizabethan times, on each side of the stage.

The costuming of plays in Gay's era was a haphazard business at best. Up to 1760 there was almost no attempt made to achieve historical accuracy in dressing the characters. There were special costumes for Shakespearian plays, but there were no firm rules, and Hotspur might appear in a wig or Macbeth in a fashionable waistcoat and breeches. There were also modified Roman costumes for classical tragedy and some extraordinarily opulent garments for Eastern potentates. Also, certain traditions were followed, such as the plume of feathers and full wig for kings and generals, the black wigs and chalked faces for murderers and conspirators, and a black velvet gown with a train carried by a page for queens of tragedy. Comedies, however, were quite another matter; they were usually costumed, as was *The Beggar's Opera,* in the most fashionable clothing of the period.

The general trends in the acting of the early eighteenth century were quite stylized. It was not until David Garrick's star rose upon the London stage in 1741 that the trend changed, for Garrick was to revolutionize the theatre with his new and natural mode of acting. In 1728, when *The Beggar's Opera* opened, the actor had little opportunity to vary the standard patterns, for tragic pieces were played always in a heavy, bombastic style and comedies were either purely farcical or "genteel." Although *The Beggar's Opera* might be considered a farce by modern standards, the elegant language which Gay put into the mouths of his underworld characters shows that the playwright intended the ballad opera to be played in the "genteel" manner, with much of the humor coming from the contrast between the coarse lines and the "refined" speakers.

John Rich, assisted by Gay, assembled a cast made up of seasoned professionals as well as obscure players for the first production of *The Beggar's Opera*. Fortunately, the cast was capable of good teamwork, a point especially important because of the unprecedented long run of the play and because of the sudden fame that was soon to fall on a number of the cast members. Particularly fortunate was the choice of Lavina Fenton as Polly Peachum. She had been added to Rich's company principally for the role of Cherry in *The Beaux' Stratagem,* and when Rich chose her for Polly, he raised her wages from fifteen to thirty shillings a week, still a mere pittance for one who was soon to become the toast of London.

Miss Fenton, said to be the best theatrical singer of her day, had been given musical training by her stepfather. At twenty, she was possessed with more than enough vocal talent, physical grace, and winsome personality to make London fall in love with her. Night after night the forty-three-year-old Duke of Bolton, Charles Powlett, paid court to Polly. At the end of the opera's run he made her his wife, ending her career as a promising actress and also distorting the ambitions of most of the ingénue actresses in London. Contemporary reports tell us that the Duke lost his heart when Polly sang "Oh, ponder well." During the high-tide of the popularity of *The Beggar's Opera,* engravings of the beauteous Polly were sold in great numbers, her biography was published, along with a book of her sayings and jests, children were named for her, and ballads were written to her. An early theatrical memoir states that "so painfully was she importuned and pursued by her numerous lovers, that it was deemed expedient that some confidential friends should guard her nightly home, to prevent her being hurt by the crowd or run away with."

Although Thomas Walker, who played Macheath in the original production, did not receive the acclaim in the press that was accorded Miss Fenton, he became the hero of the young rakes of London and was honored in the taverns and places of amusement. The role was at first given to James Quin, a celebrated actor of that day and a close friend of Gay. It was evident from the beginning, however, that Quin, who knew his inability to sing, was unhappy in the role. An early theatrical memoir tells the story that Quin heard Walker humming some of the music behind the scenes and said to Gay, "Aye, there's the man who is much more qualified to do you justice than I am." When Walker was tried out for the part, both Rich and Gay saw at once that he was a better Macheath than Quin. Already a successful actor, though not yet famous, Walker used brilliant acting to compensate for a mediocre singing voice and win a much-deserved acclaim. Contemporaries praised the "easy and dissolute air" with which Walker invested the role.

Some of the minor roles were singled out for praise during the opera's original run. John Hippisley, formerly a candle-snuffer in the theatre, was an excellent Peachum. John Hall's portrayal of Lockit also received much applause. Other members of the original cast, as given in the first printed edition of Gay's work, were: Filch, *Clark;* Jemmy Twitcher, *H. Bullock;* Crook-fingered Jack, *Houghton;* Wat Dreary, *Smith;* Robin of Bagshot, *Eaton;* Matt of the Mint, *Spiller;* Ben Budge, *Morgan;* Beggar, *Chapman;* Player, *Milward;* Mrs. Peachum, *Mrs. Martin;* Lucy Lockit, *Mrs. Egleton;* Diana Trapes, *Mrs. Martin;* Mrs. Coaxer, *Mrs. Holliday;* Dolly Trull, *Mrs. Lacy;* Mrs. Vixen, *Mrs. Rice;* Betty Doxy, *Mrs. Rogers;* Jenny Diver, *Mrs. Clarke;* Mrs. Slammekin, *Mrs. Morgan;* Suky Tawdry, *Mrs. Palin;* and Molly Brazen, *Mrs. Sallee.*

John Gay and his friends must have had many misgivings as they waited for the curtain to open at six o'clock on that cold winter evening of January 29, 1728. A subtle change had come over the theatre audiences of the early eighteenth century, making them exceed-

ingly hard to please. One of the reasons is the new taste
brought to the theatre by the rise of the middle classes,
who came to ape the follies of the nobly born. In this era
of theatrical history, the Royal Court had lost interest in
the theatre: Queen Anne rarely went to a public playhouse, and her successors, the Georges, followed her
example. Therefore the playwright could not be assured
of a discriminating audience made up of courtiers, but
had to be content with play-goers who came to the
theatre for a social occasion and to mock the author and
damn his tragedy or comedy whether it was good or bad.
A typical purveyor of this attitude was the character
Grinly in Charles Boadens's comedy, *The Modish
Couple* (1732). Grinly boasted: "I will wager you now
five hundred pounds that half a score of us shall quite
demolish the best piece that come on any stage."
Grinly's methods were simple and direct; he and his
fellows would strike up such a "chorus of cat-calls,
whistles, hisses, hoops, and horse-laughs, that not one
of the audience could hear a syllable." But theatre-goers
like Grinly in the "fop's corner" of Lincoln's Inn Fields
Theatre were in for a surprise that January night, and,
though they came to scoff, they remained to praise. And
the praise and applause has not yet ceased for Gay's
truly remarkable and long-lived ballad opera.

SYNOPSIS OF SCENES

The action recounts a series of events that take place on a single day in London in 1728.

ACT I

SCENES 1–13. Peachum's house.

ACT II

SCENES 1–6. A tavern near Newgate Prison, immediately following.
SCENES 7–9. Newgate Prison, immediately following.
SCENES 10–11. Lockit's room at Newgate Prison, immediately following.
SCENES 12–15. Another part of the prison, a few minutes later.

ACT III

SCENES 1–3. Newgate Prison, perhaps an hour later.
SCENE 4. A gaming-house, immediately following.
SCENES 5–6. Peachum's lock, about three hours later.
SCENES 7–17. Newgate Prison, perhaps an hour later.

CAST OF CHARACTERS

Men

PEACHUM, *a receiver of stolen goods.*
LOCKIT, *the jailor at Newgate Prison.*
MACHEATH, *a gentleman-highwayman.*
FILCH, *a young pickpocket.*

JEMMY TWITCHER
CROOK-FINGERED JACK
WAT DREARY
ROBIN OF BAGSHOT
NIMMING NED } *Macheath's gang*
HARRY PADINGTON
MATT OF THE MINT
BEN BUDGE

BEGGAR, *who poses in the prologue as the author of the play.*
PLAYER, *who is also in the prologue.*

Women

MRS. PEACHUM, *Polly's mother.*
POLLY PEACHUM, *who is in love with Macheath.*
LUCY LOCKIT, *daughter of the jailor; she is also in love with Macheath.*
DIANA TRAPES, *clothier to the ladies of the underworld.*

MRS. COAXER
DOLLY TRULL
MRS. VIXEN
BETTY DOXY } *Women of the town*
JENNY DIVER
MRS. SLAMMEKIN
SUKY TAWDRY
MOLLY BRAZEN

ALSO *constables, turnkeys, and a group of rabble.*

POLLY

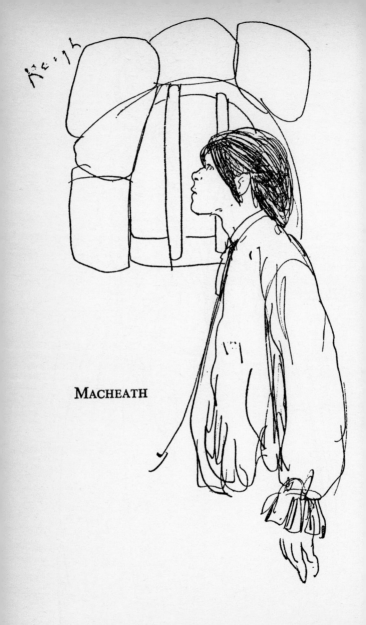

MACHEATH

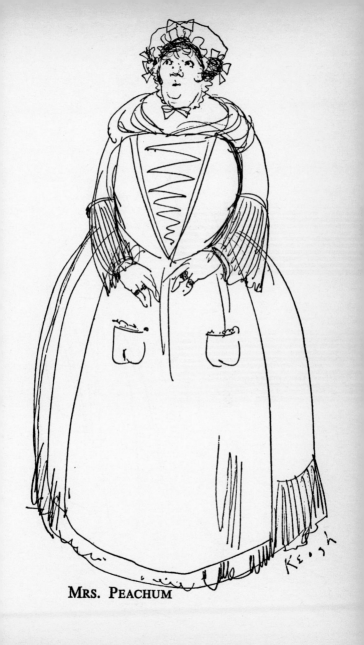

MRS. PEACHUM

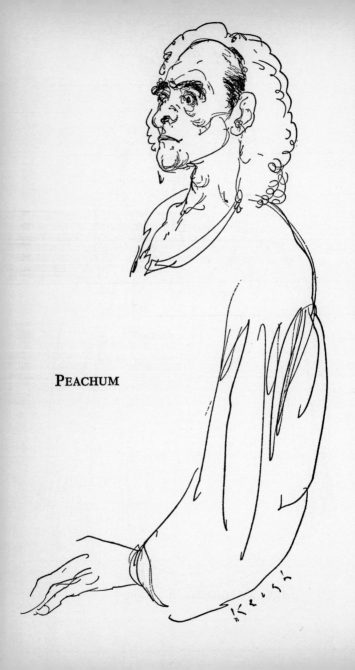

PEACHUM

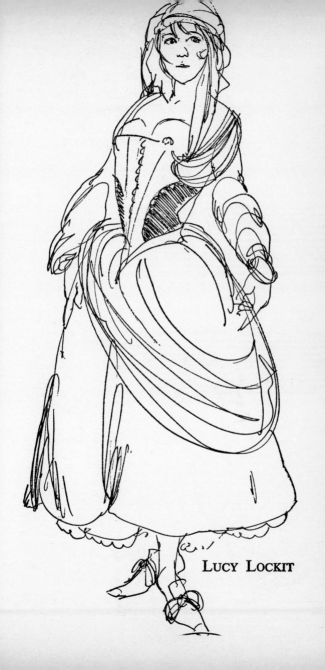

LUCY LOCKIT

LOCKIT

INTRODUCTION

Two figures part the curtain and emerge. One of them, the Beggar, is dirty and disheveled. His three-cornered hat, made of aged and shedding beaver, is pulled low over his ears. His stockings are filled with holes, and one of them is at half-mast. He wears a frowsy frock coat which is several inches long at the sleeves and which comes below his knees. The Player, by contrast, is dressed in foppish splendor. He carries his velvet cocked hat under his arm; his Ramillies wig, powdered a brilliant white, has a queue down the back. He wears tight-fitting breeches and silk stockings, and beneath his well-tailored frock coat, he wears a frilled shirt and a silk brocaded vest of mingled scarlet hues. They walk to the front of the stage; the Beggar is orating grandly.

BEGGAR: If poverty be a title to poetry, I am sure nobody can dispute mine. I own myself of the company of beggars, and I make one at their weekly festivals at St. Giles's.[1] I have a small yearly salary for my catches [2] and am welcome to a dinner there whenever I please, which is more than most poets can say.

PLAYER: As we live by the muses,[3] it is but gratitude in us to encourage poetical merit wherever we find it. The muses, contrary to all other ladies, pay no distinction to dress, and never partially mistake the pertness of embroidery for wit, nor the modesty of want for dullness. Be the author who he will, we push his play as far as it will go. So (though you are in want) I wish you success heartily.

BEGGAR: This piece, I own, was originally writ for the celebrating the marriage of James Chanter and Moll Lay, two most excellent ballad-singers. I have introduced the similes that are in you celebrated operas: the Swallow, the Moth, the Bee, the Ship, the Flower, etc. Besides, I have a prison-scene, which the ladies always reckon charmingly pathetic. As to the parts, I have observed such a nice impartiality to our two ladies,[4] that it is impossible for either of them to take offence. I hope I may be forgiven, that I have not made my opera throughout unnatural, like those in vogue; for I have no recitative: excepting this, as I have consented to have neither prologue nor epilogue, it must be allowed an opera in all its forms. The piece indeed hath been heretofore frequently represented by ourselves in our great room at St. Giles's, so that I cannot too often acknowledge your charity in bringing it now on the stage.

PLAYER: But I see 'tis time for us to withdraw; the actors are preparing to begin. Play away the overture. *They go out hastily.*

ACT I

Scene One

The place is London, early in the eighteenth century;
the scene is Peachum's house. It is mid-morning, and as
the curtain opens Peachum is seen seated at a table,
poring over a large book of accounts. He is a tall, lean
man like Cassius, whom Shakespeare's Julius Cæsar
described as "dangerous." His black, piercing eyes de-
note intelligence. From his bearing one might easily
imagine Peachum as a prime minister or a chief justice
rather than as the predatory manipulator of the London
underworld that he is. He wears his ill-fitting, powdered
wig on the back of his head, revealing his baldness. His

61

white shirt has long, full sleeves; his tight-fitting black breeches and black stockings contrast with his billowing blouse, accentuating his leanness. His black shoes are unbuckled for comfort. After a few moments he throws down his quill pen and begins to sing in a deep bass voice.

> AIR I—An old woman clothed in gray, etc.[1]
> *Through all the employments of life,*
> *Each neighbor abuses his brother;*
> *Whore and rogue they call husband and wife:*
> *All professions be-rogue one another.*
> *The priest calls the lawyer a cheat,*
> *The lawyer be-knaves the divine;*
> *And the statesman, because he's so great,*
> *Thinks his trade as honest as mine.*

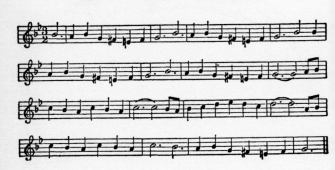

A lawyer is an honest employment; so is mine. Like me, too, he acts in a double capacity, both against rogues and for 'em; for 'tis but fitting that we should protect and encourage cheats, since we live by 'em.

Scene Two [2]

Peachum returns to his account books as Filch walks briskly on stage from the right. Filch, thin and tousle-headed, is a saucy young delinquent of about nineteen. His agility of movement indicates the muscular co-ordination that has made him the leading apprentice pickpocket of the Peachum gang. He wears a puffy white

blouse carelessly tucked into his tight gray breeches.
His white stockings have fallen down over his high-
heeled, buckled slippers. He speaks excitedly.

FILCH: Sir, Black Moll hath sent word her trial comes
on in the afternoon, and she hopes you will order
matters so as to bring her off.

PEACHUM: (*with professional aplomb*) Why, she
may plead her belly [3] at worst; to my knowledge she
hath taken care of that security. But as the wench is
very active and industrious, you may satisfy her that
I'll soften the evidence.

FILCH: (*somewhat timidly*) Tom Gagg, sir, is found
guilty.

PEACHUM: (*angrily*) A lazy dog! When I took him
the time before, I told him what he would come to if he
did not mend his hand. This is death without reprieve.
I may venture to book him. (*He writes in his account
book, mouthing the words as he pens them.*) For Tom
Gagg, forty pounds. Let Betty Sly know that I'll save her
from transportation, for I can get more by her staying in
England.

FILCH: Betty hath brought more goods into our lock [4]
to-year, than any five of the gang; and in truth, 'tis a
pity to lose so good a customer. [5]

PEACHUM: (*heartily*) If none of the gang take her
off, she may, in the common course of business, live a
twelve-month longer. I love to let women 'scape. A good
sportsman always lets the hen partridges fly, because the
breed of the game depends upon them. Besides, here
the law allows us no reward; there is nothing to be got
by the death of women—except our wives.

FILCH: (*his eyes lighting up*) Without dispute, she
is a fine woman! 'Twas to her I was obliged for my
education, and (to say a bold word) she hath trained up
more young fellows to the business than the gaming-
table.

PEACHUM: Truly, Filch, thy observation is right. We
and the surgeons are more beholden to women than all
the professions besides.

FILCH: (*singing in a high, poignant tenor*)

AIR II—The bonny gray-eyed morn, etc.
'Tis woman that seduces all mankind,
    By her we first were taught the wheedling arts;
Her very eyes can cheat: when most she's kind,
    She tricks us of our money with our hearts.
For her, like wolves by night we roam for prey,
    And practice every fraud to bribe her charms;
For suits of love, like law, are won by pay,
    And beauty must be fee'd into our arms.

PEACHUM: (*grandly*) But make haste to Newgate,[6] boy, and let my friends know what I intend; for I love to make them easy one way or other.

FILCH: (*comically philosophical*) When a gentleman is long kept in suspense, penitence may break his spirit ever after. Besides, certainty gives a man a good air upon his trail, and makes him risk another without fear or scruple. But I'll away, for 'tis a pleausre to be the messenger of comfort to friends in affliction. (*He hurries off stage to the right.*)

Scene Three

PEACHUM: But 'tis now high time to look about me for a decent execution against next sessions.[7] I hate a lazy rogue, by whom one can get nothing till he is hanged. A register of the gang: (*reading aloud*) "Crook-fingered Jack. A year and a half in the service." Let me see how much the stock owes to his industry; one, two, three, four, five gold watches, and seven silver ones.—A mighty clean-handed fellow!—Sixteen snuff-boxes, five of them of true gold. Six dozen of handkerchiefs, four silver-hilted swords, half a dozen of shirts, three tie-periwigs, and a piece of broadcloth. —Considering these are only the fruits of his leisure hours, I don't know a prettier fellow, for no man alive hath a more engaging presence of mind upon the road.[8] "Wat Dreary, alias Brown Will"—an irregular dog, who hath an underhand way of disposing of his goods. I'll try him only for a sessions or two longer upon his good behavior. "Harry Padington"—a poor petty-larceny rascal, without the least genius; that fellow, though he were to live these six months, will never come to the gallows with any credit. "Slippery Sam"—he goes off the next sessions, for the villain hath the impudence to have views of following his trade as a tailor, which he calls an honest employment. "Matt of the Mint"—listed not above a month ago, a promising sturdy fellow, and diligent in his way: somewhat too bold and hasty, and may raise good contributions on the public, if he does not cut himself short by murder. "Tom Tipple"—a guzzling, soaking sot, who is always too drunk to stand himself, or to make others stand. A cart [9] is absolutely necessary for him. "Robin of Bagshot, alias Gorgon, alias Bluff Bob, alias Carbuncle, alias Bob Booty!—" [10]

Scene Four

Mrs. Peachum, a huge, unpleasingly plump woman, enters quietly from the right and gyrates her great body with tiny steps toward her husband. Together, the pair resembles Jack Spratt and his overweight spouse. She wears a white lace cap with bows at the sides and on top. Her pink skirt is of the hoop type which Sir Roger de Coverley compared to a gocart; it is rounded in the shape of a cupola. The bottom halves of her loose-

fitting sleeves are a brilliant red. She wears four large and ostentatious rings on her fat fingers. Her hair is a bright carrot-red.

MRS. PEACHUM: (*kittenishly*) What of Bob Booty, husband? I hope nothing bad hath betided him. You know, my dear, he's a favorite customer of mine. 'Twas he made me a present of this ring. (*She holds up the ring on her right little finger and looks at it admiringly.*)

PEACHUM: (*curt and business-like*) I have set his name down in the black list, that's all, my dear; he spends his life among women, and as soon as his money is gone, one or other of the ladies will hang him for the reward, and there's forty pound lost to us forever.

MRS. PEACHUM: (*still admiring her rings*) You know, my dear, I never meddle in matters of death; I always leave those affairs to you. Women indeed are bitter bad judges in these cases, for they are so partial to the brave that they think every man handsome who is going to the camp [11] or the gallows. (*She begins to sing in a creaking contralto.*)

AIR III—Cold and raw, etc.
If any wench Venus's girdle wear,
  Though she be never so ugly,
Lilies and roses will quickly appear,
  And her face look wondrous smugly.
Beneath the left ear so fit but a cord,
  (A rope so charming a zone is!)
The youth in his cart hath the air of a lord,
  And we cry, There dies an Adonis!

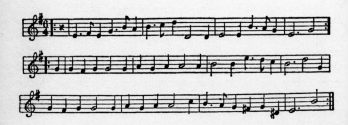

But really, husband, you should not be too hard-hearted, for you never had a finer, braver set of men than at present. We have not had a murder among them all, these seven months. And truly, my dear, that is a great blessing.

PEACHUM: (*blusteringly*) What a dickens is the woman always a-whimp'ring about murder for? No gentleman is ever looked upon the worse for killing a man in his own defence; and if business cannot be carried on without it, what would you have a gentleman do?

MRS. PEACHUM: (*attempting to calm him*) If I am in the wrong, my dear, you must excuse me, for nobody can help the frailty of an over-scrupulous conscience.

PEACHUM: (*waxing oratorical*) Murder is as fashionable a crime as a man can be guilty of. How many fine gentlemen have we in Newgate every year, purely upon that article! If they have wherewithal to persuade the jury to bring it in manslaughter, what are they the worse for it? So my dear, have done upon this subject. (*turning suddenly to another matter*) Was Captain Macheath here this morning, for the bank-notes he left with you last week?

MRS. PEACHUM: (*gushingly*) Yes, my dear; and though the bank has stopped payment, he was so cheerful and so agreeable! Sure there is not a finer gentleman upon the road than the captain! If he comes from Bagshot at any reasonable hour he hath promised to make one this evening with Polly and me, and Bob Booty, at a party of quadrille. Pray, my dear, is the captain rich?

PEACHUM: (*pompously*) The captain keeps too good company ever to grow rich. Marybone [12] and the chocolate-houses are his undoing. The man that proposes to get money by play should have the education of a fine gentleman, and be trained up to it from his youth.

MRS. PEACHUM: (*genuinely upset*) Really, I am sorry upon Polly's account the captain hath not more discretion. What business hath he to keep company with lords and gentlemen? he should leave them to prey upon one another.

PEACHUM: (*aroused*) Upon Polly's account! What a plague does the woman mean?—Upon Polly's account!

MRS. PEACHUM: Captain Macheath is very fond of the girl.

PEACHUM: And what then?

MRS. PEACHUM: (*becoming intimidated*) If I have any skill in the ways of women, I am sure Polly thinks him a very pretty man.

PEACHUM: (*now angry*) And what then? You would not be so mad to have the wench marry him! Gamesters and highwaymen are generally very good to their whores, but they are very devils to their wives.

MRS. PEACHUM: (*disturbed*) But if Polly should be in love, how should we help her, or how can she help herself? Poor girl, I am in the utmost concern about her. (*She paces about and begins to sing plaintively.*)

AIR IV—Why is your faithful slave disdained? etc.
> *If love the virgin's heart invade,*
> *How, like a moth, the simple maid*
> * Still plays about the flame!*
> *If soon she be not made a wife,*
> *Her honour's singed, and then, for life,*
> *She's—what I dare not name.*

PEACHUM: (*controlling his anger*) Look ye, wife. A handsome wench in our way of business is as profitable as at the bar of a Temple [13] coffee house, who looks upon it as her livelihood to grant every liberty but one.

You see I would indulge the girl as far as prudently we can,—in anything but marriage! After that, my dear, how shall we be safe? Are we not then in her husband's power? For a husband hath the absolute power over all a wife's secrets but her own. If the girl had the discretion of a court lady, who can have a dozen young fellows at her ear without complying with one, I should not matter it; but Polly is a tinder, and a spark will at once set her on a flame. Married! If the wench does not know her own profit, sure she knows her own pleasure better than to make herself a property! My daughter to me should be, like a court lady to a minister of state, a key to the whole gang. Married! if the affair is not already done, I'll terrify her from it, by the example of our neighbors.

MRS. PEACHUM: (*trying to mollify him*) Mayhap, my dear, you may injure the girl. She loves to imitate the fine ladies, and she may only allow the captain liberties in the view of interest.

PEACHUM: (*preparing to leave*) But 'tis your duty, my dear, to warn the girl against her ruin, and to instruct her how to make the most of her beauty. I'll go to her this moment, and sift her. In the meantime, wife, rip out the coronets and marks of these dozen cambric handkerchiefs, for I can dispose of them this afternoon to a chap [14] in the city. (*He hastens off stage to the right.*)

Scene Five

MRS. PEACHUM: (*thoughtfully*) Never was a man more out of the way in an argument than my husband! Why must our Polly, forsooth, differ from her sex, and love only her husband? And why must Polly's marriage, contrary to all observation, make her the less followed by other men? All men are thieves in love, and like a woman the better for being another's property.

> AIR V—Of all the simple things we do, etc.
> *A maid is like the golden ore,*
> *Which hath guineas intrinsical in't;*

Whose worth is never known, before
It is tried and impressed in the mint.
A wife's like a guinea in gold,
Stamped with the name of her spouse;
Now here, now there; is bought, or is sold;
And is current in every house.

Scene Six

Filch enters from the right, laden with articles he has stolen.

MRS. PEACHUM: (*affectionately*) Come hither, Filch. I am as fond of this child as though my mind misgave me he were my own. He hath as fine a hand at picking a pocket as a woman, and is as nimble-fingered as a juggler. If an unlucky session does not cut the rope of thy life, I pronounce, boy, thou wilt be a great man in history. Where was your post last night, my boy?

FILCH: (*in high spirits*) I plied at the opera, madam; and considering 'twas neither dark nor rainy, so that there was no great hurry in getting chairs and coaches, made a tolerable hand on't. These seven handkerchiefs, madam.

MRS. PEACHUM: (*appraising them expertly*) Colored ones, I see. They are of sure sale from our warehouse at Redriff [15] among the seamen.

FILCH: (*proudly*) And this snuff-box.

MRS. PEACHUM: Set in gold! A pretty encouragement this to a young beginner.

FILCH: (*enthusiastically*) I had a fair tug at a charming gold watch. Pox take the tailors for making the fobs so deep and narrow. It stuck by the way, and I was forced to make my escape under a coach. (*He becomes suddenly serious.*) Really, madam, I fear, I shall be cut off in the flower of my youth, so that every now and then (since I was pumped) [16] I have thoughts of taking up and going to sea.

MRS. PEACHUM: (*consolingly*) You should go to Hockley-in-the-Hole [17] and to Marybone, child, to learn valor. These are the schools that have bred so many brave men. I thought, boy, by this time, thou hadst lost fear as well as shame.—Poor lad! how little does he know as yet of the Old Bailey! [18] For the first fact I'll insure thee from being hanged; and going to sea, Filch, will come time enough upon a sentence of transportation. But now, since you have nothing better to do, even go to your book, and learn your catechism; for really a man makes but an ill figure in the ordinary's paper,[19] who cannot give a satisfactory answer to his questions. But, hark you, my lad. Don't tell me a lie; for you know I hate a liar. Do you know of anything that hath passed between Captain Macheath and our Polly?

FILCH: (*fearfully*) I beg you madam, don't ask me; for I must either tell a lie to you or to Miss Polly—for I promised her I would not tell.

MRS. PEACHUM: But when the honor of our family is concerned—

FILCH: I shall lead a sad life with Miss Polly if ever she come to know that I told you. Besides, I would not willingly forfeit my own honor by betraying anybody.

MRS. PEACHUM: (*patting Filch lightly on the shoulder*) Yonder comes my husband and Polly. Come, Filch, you shall go with me into my own room, and tell me the whole story. I'll give thee a glass of a most delicious cordial that I keep for my own drinking. (*They go out, stage left, her arm about his shoulder.*)

Scene Seven

Polly Peachum, an island of relative artlessness and innocence in a sea of infamy, enters at the right of the stage with her father. Her beauty is reminiscent of Hogarth's painting of the shrimp girl. There is a trace of sadness in her large blue eyes. Her auburn hair peeps from her white lace cap in delightful disorder, but her light-blue dress is of the latest fashion, with a hoop skirt accenting her trim waist. She wears a long white apron in the newest fashion, lending an air of domesticity to her appearance. Peachum's face is set in a stern mask of parental disapproval.

POLLY: I know as well as any of the fine ladies how to make the most of myself and of my man too. A woman knows how to be mercenary, though she hath never been in a court or at an assembly. We have it in our natures, papa. If I allow Captain Macheath some trifling liberties, I have this watch and other visible marks of his favor to show for it. A girl who cannot grant some things, and refuse what is most material, will make but a poor hand of her beauty, and soon be thrown upon the common. (*She walks slowly toward the apron of the stage and begins to sing.*)

AIR VI—What shall I do to show how much I love her, etc.
> Virgins are like the fair flower in its lustre,
>   Which in the garden enamels the ground;
> Near it the bees in play flutter and cluster,
>   And gaudy butterflies frolic around.
> But, when once plucked, 'tis no longer alluring;
>   To Covent-garden [20] 'tis sent (as yet sweet),
> There fades, and shrinks, and grows past all enduring,
>   Rots, stinks, and dies, and is trod under feet.

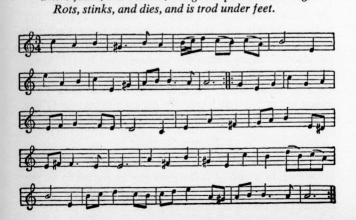

PEACHUM: (*carefully controlling his emotions*) You know, Polly, I am not against your toying and trifling with a customer in the way of business, or to get out a secret or so. But if I find out that you have played the fool and are married (*grasping her arm roughly and giving full vent to his anger*), you jade you, I'll cut your throat, hussy! Now you know my mind.

Scene Eight

Mrs. Peachum, having learned Polly's secret from Filch, bursts onto the stage from the left. She is in a state of high dudgeon and immediately begins pouring out her anger in song.

AIR VII—Oh London is a fine town.
Our Polly is a sad slut! nor heeds what we have taught her.
I wonder any man alive will ever rear a daughter!
For she must have both hoods and gowns, and hoops to swell her pride,
With scarfs and stays, and gloves and lace; and she will have men beside;
And when she's dressed with care and cost, all-tempting fine and gay,
As men should serve a cowcumber,[21] *she flings herself away.*

(*She turns on Polly and grasps her roughly by the wrist.*)
You baggage, you hussy! you inconsiderate jade! Had you been hanged, it would not have vexed me, for that might have been your misfortune; but to do such a mad thing by choice! The wench is married, husband.

PEACHUM: (*exploding*) Married! The captain is a bold man, and will risk anything for money; to be sure, he believes her a fortune!—Do you think your mother and I should have lived comfortably so long together, **if** ever we had been married? Baggage!

MRS. PEACHUM: (*turning her back on Polly, her arms folded*) I knew she was always a proud slut; **and** now the wench hath played the fool and married because, forsooth, she would do like the gentry. Can you support the expense of a husband, hussy, in gaming, drinking, and whoring? Have you money enough to carry on the daily quarrels of man and wife about who shall squander most? There are not many husbands and wives who can bear the charges of plaguing one another in a handsome way. If you must be married, could you introduce nobody into our family but a highwayman? Why, thou foolish jade, thou wilt be as ill used, and as much neglected, as if thou hadst married a lord!

PEACHUM: (*becoming less emotional*) Let not your anger, my dear, break through the rules of decency, for the captain looks upon himself in the military capacity, as a gentleman by his profession. Besides what he hath already, I know he is in a fair way of getting, or of dying; and both these ways, let me tell you, are most excellent chances for a wife.—Tell me, hussy, are you ruined or no?

MRS. PEACHUM: (*petulantly*) With Polly's fortune, she might very well have gone off to a person of distinction. (*She boils over with anger again.*) Yes, that you might, you pouting slut!
Polly is now kneeling, her head resting on her left arm, her eyes closed.

PEACHUM: (*bending near Polly's ear and shouting*) What, is the wench dumb? Speak, or I'll make you plead by squeezing out an answer from you. Are you really bound wife to him, or are you only upon liking? (*He pinches her.*)

POLLY: (*screaming*) Oh!

MRS. PEACHUM: (*railing*) How the mother is to be pitied who hath handsome daughters! Locks, bolts, bars, and lectures of morality are nothing to them; they break through them all. They have as much pleasure in cheat-

ing a father and mother as in cheating at cards.

PEACHUM: Why, Polly, I shall soon know if you are married, by Macheath's keeping from our house.

POLLY: (*still kneeling, her hands folded in a beseeching attitude, she begins to sing tenderly*)

> *AIR VIII*—Grim king of ghosts, etc.
> *Can love be controlled by advice?*
> *Will Cupid our mothers obey?*
> *Though my heart were as frozen as ice,*
>   *At his flame 'twould have melted away.*
>
> *When he kissed me, so closely he pressed,*
>   *'Twas so sweet that I must have complied,*
> *So I thought it both safest and best*
>   *To marry, for fear you should chide.*

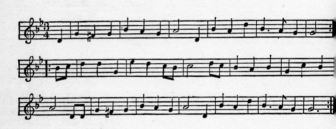

MRS. PEACHUM: (*incredulously*) Then all the hopes of our family are gone for ever and ever!

PEACHUM: (*shaking his head querulously*) And Macheath may hang his father- and mother-in-law, in hope to get into their daughter's fortune!

POLLY: (*staunchly*) I did not marry him (as 'tis the fashion) coolly and deliberately for honor or money— but I love him.

MRS. PEACHUM: (*violently agitated*) Love him! Worse and worse! I thought the girl had been better bred. O husband, husband! her folly makes me mad! my head swims! I'm distracted! I can't support myself— Oh! (*Mrs. Peachum faints, collapsing into a great mound of flesh and petticoats on the floor.*)

PEACHUM: (*kneeling beside his wife and massaging her wrists*) See, wench, to what condition you have reduced your poor mother! a glass of cordial, this instant. How the poor woman takes it to heart! (*Polly goes out, stage right, and returns immediately with a glass of wine.*) Ah, hussy, now this is the only comfort your mother has left!

POLLY: (*genuinely disturbed*) Give her another glass, sir; my mama drinks double the quantity whenever she is out of order.—This, you see, fetches her.

MRS. PEACHUM: (*rallying*) The girl shows such a readiness, and so much concern, that I could almost find in my heart to forgive her. (*She raises herself on one elbow and begins to sing plaintively.*)

> AIR IX—O Jenny, O Jenny, where hast thou been.
> *O Polly, you might have toyed and kissed;*
> *By keeping men off, you keep them on.*
> POLLY: *But he so teased me,*
> *And he so pleased me,*
> *What I did, you must have done—*

MRS. PEACHUM: (*disdainfully*) Not with a highwayman.—You sorry slut!

PEACHUM: (*again calm and philosophical*) A word with you, wife. 'Tis no new thing for a wench to take man without consent of her parents. You know 'tis the frailty of woman, my dear.

MRS. PEACHUM: (*becoming more tranquil*) Yes, indeed, the sex is frail. But the first time a woman is frail, she should be somewhat nice, methinks, for then or never is the time to make her fortune. After that, she hath nothing to do but to guard herself from being found out, and she may do what she pleases.

PEACHUM: (*smiling enigmatically*) Make yourself a little easy; I have a thought shall soon set all matters again to rights. Why so melancholy, Polly? Since what is done cannot be undone, we must all endeavor to make the best of it.

MRS. PEACHUM: (*putting her arm around Polly's waist*) Well, Polly, as far as one woman can forgive another, I forgive thee.—Your father is too fond of you, hussy.

POLLY: (*hopefully*) Then all my sorrows are at an end.

MRS. PEACHUM: (*somewhat acidly*) A mighty likely speech in troth, for a wench who is just married.

POLLY: (*smiling as she sings*)

> AIR X—Thomas, I cannot, etc.
> I, like a ship in storms, was tossed,
>   Yet afraid to put into land;
> For seized in the port, the vessel's lost,
>   Whose treasure is contraband.
>   The waves are laid,
>   My duty's paid,
>   Oh, joy beyond expression!
>   Thus, safe ashore,
>   I ask no more,
>   My all is in my possession.

PEACHUM: (*cupping his hand to his ear*) I hear customers in t'other room. Go, talk with 'em, Polly; but come to us again as soon as they are gone.—But, hark ye, child, if 'tis the gentleman who was here yesterday about the repeating watch, say, you believe we can't get intelligence of it till to-morrow—for I lent it to Suky Straddle, to make a figure with to-night at a tavern in Drury Lane. If t'other gentleman calls for the silver-hilted sword, you know beetle-browed Jemmy hath it on, and he doth not come from Tunbridge [22] till Tuesday night; so that it cannot be had till then.

Polly goes out dutifully to the right.

Scene Nine

PEACHUM: (*looking to be certain that Polly is out of earshot*) Dear wife, be a little pacified. Don't let your passion run away with your senses. Polly, I grant you, hath done a rash thing.

MRS. PEACHUM: (*still wringing her hands*) If she had had only an intrigue with the fellow, why, the very best families have excused and huddled up a frailty of that sort. 'Tis marriage, husband, that makes it a blemish.

PEACHUM: (*placatingly*) But money, wife, is the true fuller's earth [23] for reputations; there is not a spot or a stain but what it can take out. A rich rogue nowadays is fit company for any gentleman, and the world, my dear, hath not such contempt for roguery as you imagine. I tell you, wife, I can make this match turn to our advantage.

MRS. PEACHUM: I am very sensible, husband, that Captain Macheath is worth money, but I am in doubt whether he hath not two or three wives already, and then if he should die in a session or two, Polly's dower would come into dispute.

PEACHUM: That, indeed, is a point which ought to be considered.

(*He assumes a thoughtful pose for a few moments and then strolls toward the front of the stage and begins to sing.*)

> AIR XI—A soldier and a sailor.
> *A fox may steal your hens, sir,*
> *A whore your health and pence, sir,*
> *Your daughter rob your chest, sir,*

Your wife may steal your rest, sir,
  A thief your goods and plate.
But this is all but picking;
With rest, pence, chest, and chicken;
It ever was decreed, sir,
If lawyer's hand is fee'd, sir,
  He steals your whole estate.

The lawyers are bitter enemies to those in our way. They don't care that anybody should get a clandestine livelihood but themselves.

Scene Ten

Polly enters from the right.

POLLY: 'Twas only Nimming Ned.[24] He brought in a damask window-curtain, a hoop petticoat, a pair of silver candlesticks, a periwig, and one silk stocking, from the fire that happened last night.

PEACHUM: (*delighted*) There is not a fellow that is cleverer in his way and saves more goods out of the fire, than Ned. (*becoming more serious*) But now,

Polly, to your affair; for matters must not be left as they are. You are married then, it seems?

POLLY: (*hanging her head*) Yes, sir.

PEACHUM: And how do you propose to live, child?

POLLY: Like other women, sir,—upon the industry of my husband.

MRS. PEACHUM: (*again irate*) What, is the wench turned fool? A highwayman's wife, like a soldier's, hath as little of his pay as of his company.

PEACHUM: And had not you the common views of a gentlewoman in your marriage, Polly?

POLLY: (*innocently*) I don't know what you mean, sir.

PEACHUM: Of a jointure,[25] and of being a widow.

POLLY: But I love him, sir; how then could I have thoughts of parting with him?

PEACHUM: (*becoming impatient*) Parting with him! Why, that is the whole scheme and intention of all marriage articles. The comfortable estate of widowhood is the only hope that keeps up a wife's spirits. Where is the woman who would scruple to be a wife, if she had it in her power to be a widow whenever she pleased? If you have any views of this sort, Polly, I shall think the match not so very unreasonable.

POLLY: (*perturbed*) How I dread to hear your advice! Yet I must beg you to explain yourself.

PEACHUM: Secure what he hath got, have him peached[26] the next sessions, and then at once you are made a rich widow.

POLLY: (*utterly distracted*) What, murder the man I love! The blood runs cold at my heart with the very thought of it.

PEACHUM: (*coldly and analytically*) Fie, Polly! What hath murder to do in the affair? Since the thing sooner or later must happen, I dare say the captain himself would like that we should get the reward for his death sooner than a stranger. Why, Polly, the captain knows that as 'tis his employment to rob, so 'tis ours to take robbers; every man in his business. So that there is no malice in the case.

MRS. PEACHUM: Ay, husband, now you have nicked the matter. To have him peached is the only thing that could ever make me forgive her.

POLLY: (*kneeling imploringly before her parents, she begins to sing in sad, beseeching tones*)

AIR XII—Now ponder well, ye parents dear.
> *Oh, ponder well! be not severe;*
> *So save a wretched wife!*
> *For on the rope that hangs my dear*
> *Depends poor Polly's life.*

MRS. PEACHUM: But your duty to your parents, hussy, obliges you to hang him. What would many a wife give for such an opportunity!

POLLY: (*wiping a tear from her eye*) What is a jointure, what is widowhood to me? I know my heart. I cannot survive him.

AIR XIII—Le printemps rappelle aux armes.
> *The turtle thus with plaintive crying,*
> *Her lover dying,*
> *The turtle thus with plaintive crying,*
> *Laments her dove.*
> *Down she drops, quite spent with sighing;*
> *Paired in death, as paired in love.*

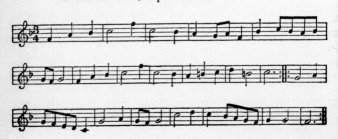

Thus, sir, it will happen to your poor Polly.

MRS. PEACHUM: What, is the fool in love in earnest then? I hate thee for being particular. Why, wench, thou art a shame to thy very sex.

POLLY: (*tearfully*) But hear me, mother,—if you ever loved—

MRS. PEACHUM: (*drawing back her hand as if to strike*) Those cursed play-books she reads have been her ruin. One word more, hussy, and I shall knock your brains out, if you have any.

PEACHUM: Keep out of the way, Polly, for fear of mischief, and consider what is proposed to you.

MRS. PEACHUM: Away, hussy! Hang your husband, and be dutiful.

Scene Eleven

Polly walks slowly to the left of the stage and stops, listening to what her parents are saying.

MRS. PEACHUM: (*arguing her case like a barrister*) The thing, husband, must and shall be done. For the sake of intelligence, we must take other measures and have him peached the next session without her consent. If she will not know her duty, we know ours.

PEACHUM: (*pursing his lips gravely*) But really, my dear, it grieves one's heart to take off a great man. When I consider his personal bravery, his fine stratagem,[27] how much we have already got by him, and how much more we may get, methinks I can't find in my heart to have a hand in his death. I wish you could have made Polly undertake it.

MRS. PEACHUM: But in a case of necessity—our own lives are in danger.

PEACHUM: (*grandly*) Then, indeed, we must comply with the customs of the world, and make gratitude give way to interest. He shall be taken off.

MRS. PEACHUM: I'll undertake to manage Polly.

PEACHUM: And I'll prepare matters for the Old Bailey.

They exit slowly, stage right, without noticing Polly.

Scene Twelve

After watching her parents go out, Polly, now wringing her hands in anguish, walks to the center of the stage.

POLLY: Now I'm a wretch, indeed—methinks I see him already in the cart, sweeter and more lovely than the nosegay in his hand!—I hear the crowd extolling his resolution and intrepidity!—What volleys of sighs are sent from the windows of Holborn,[28] that so comely a youth should be brought to disgrace!—I see him at the tree! [29]

(The vision is too much for her, and she covers her eyes with her hands.)

The whole circle are in tears!—even butchers weep!— Jack Ketch [30] himself hesitates to perform his duty, and would be glad to lose his fee, by a reprieve. What then will become of Polly? As yet I may inform him of their design, and aid him in his escape. It shall be so!—But then he flies, absents himself, and I bar myself from his dear, dear conversation!

(The gravity of the dilemma now fully realized, Polly tosses her head in bewilderment.)

That too will distract me. If he keeps out of the way, my papa and mama may in time relent, and we may be happy. If he stays, he is hanged, and then he is lost forever! He intended to lie concealed in my room till the dusk of evening. If they are abroad, I'll this instant let him out, lest some accident should prevent him. *(She hurries out to the left.)*

Scene Thirteen

Polly and Captain Macheath enter arm-in-arm from the left. Macheath is the very epitome of a gentleman-highwayman. He is tall and ruggedly handsome. This darling of the ladies and demon of the highways wears his knee-length white coat with grace and masculinity. His boots are of white kidskin; his wig of natural-colored brown hair is brushed straight back into a simple knot.

As Polly and the captain enter, they are singing a gay love duet.

MACHEATH: AIR XIV—Pretty Parrot, say.
                      Pretty Polly, say,
                      When I was away,
                      Did your fancy never stray
                      To some newer lover?

POLLY: *Without disguise,*
                      Heaving sighs,
                      Doating eyes,
                      My constant heart discover.
                      Fondly let me loll!

MACHEATH: *O pretty, pretty Poll.*

POLLY: (*anxiously*) And are *you* as fond as ever, my dear?

MACHEATH: (*oratorically*) Suspect my honor, my courage—suspect anything but my love. May my pistols miss fire, and my mare slip her shoulder while I am pursued, if I ever forsake thee!

POLLY: (*naively*) Nay, my dear, I have no reason to doubt you, for I find in the romance you lent me, none of the great heroes were ever false in love.

MACHEATH: *AIR XV*—Pray, fair one, be kind
                      My heart was so free,
                      It roved like a bee,
                 Till Polly my passion requited:
                      I sipped each flower,
                      I changed every hour,
                 But here every flower is united.

POLLY: Were you sentenced to transportation ~Australia~, sure, my dear, you could not leave me behind you,—could you?

MACHEATH: (*embracing her impulsively*) Is there any power, any force that could tear me from thee? You might sooner tear a pension out of the hands of a courtier, a fee from a lawyer, a pretty woman from a looking glass, or any woman from quadrille. But to tear me from thee is impossible!

                 AIR XVI—Over the hills and far away.
                 Were I laid on Greenland's coast,
                 And in my arms embraced my lass;
                 Warm amidst eternal frost,
                 Too soon the half year's night would pass.
POLLY: *Were I sold on Indian soil,*
                 Soon as the burning day was closed,
                 I could mock the sultry toil,
                 When on my charmer's breast reposed.
MACHEATH: *And I would love you all the day,*
POLLY: *Every night would kiss and play,*
MACHEATH: *If with me you'd fondly stray*
POLLY: *Over the hills and far away.*

POLLY: (*sadly*) Yes, I would go with thee. But oh!—how shall I speak it? I must be torn from thee. We must part.

MACHEATH: How! Part!

POLLY: (*hardly able to contain herself*) We must, we must. My papa and mama are set against thy life. They now, even now, are in search after thee. They are preparing evidence against thee. Thy life depends upon a moment.

> *AIR XVII*—'Gin thou wert mine awn thing.
> Oh, what pain it is to part!
> Can I leave thee, can I leave thee?
> Oh, what pain it is to part!
> Can thy Polly ever leave thee?
> But lest death my love should thwart
> And bring thee to the fatal cart,
> Thus I tear thee from my bleeding heart!
> Fly hence, and let me leave thee.

Fable of the Bees

One kiss and then,—one kiss. Begone,—farewell.

MACHEATH: My hand, my heart, my dear, is so riveted to thine, that I cannot unloose my hold.

POLLY: (*fearfully*) But my papa may intercept thee, and then I should lose the very glimmering of hope. A few weeks, perhaps, may reconcile us all. Shall thy Polly hear from thee?

MACHEATH: Must I then go?

POLLY: And will not absence change your love?

MACHEATH: (*nobly*) If you doubt it, let me stay— and be hanged.

POLLY: (*much agitated*) Oh, I fear! how I tremble! —Go—but when safety will give you leave, you will be sure to see me again; for till then Polly is wretched.

With difficulty, they part. They continue to look back at each other with fondness as she walks toward the left door, he the right.

MACHEATH: *AIR XVIII*—Oh the broom, etc.
            The miser thus a shilling sees,
              Which he's obliged to pay,
            With sighs resigns it by degrees,
              And fears 'tis gone for aye.

End of the first Act

POLLY: *The boy, thus, when his sparrow's flown,*
            The bird in silence eyes;
          But soon as out of sight 'tis gone,
            Whines, whimpers, sobs, and cries.

(*With heads bowed they turn and go out.*)

ACT II

Scene One

The scene is a tavern near Newgate Prison. Only a few moments have elapsed since the previous scene. The members of Macheath's gang have assembled, and though they are partaking freely of wine, brandy, and tobacco, the conversation is on a somewhat philosophical plane as they discuss the exigencies of a criminal life. The principal characters are Jemmy Twitcher, lean and tall, with a gray peaked hat resting on his acquiline nose; Crook-fingered Jack, a squat, pugnacious culprit with bushy hair; Wat Dreary, slender, ludicrously melancholy, with a pointed red nose and bleary eyes; Robin of Bagshot, who looks somewhat like an ill-dressed lord, for he is used by the playwright to satirize Sir Robert Walpole; Nimming Ned, a sad-faced, sloe-eyed old veteran who peers soulfully from beneath a large beaver hat; Harry Padington, a tall skeleton of a man with a blank, moronic expression; Matt of the Mint, described by

Peachum as "somewhat too bold and hasty" and destined to be hanged for murder, has great staring eyes that bear a glint of animal cunning; and Ben Budge, who seems younger and yet more intelligent than the others; he wears a high-peaked hat atop his disheveled mop of hair. There are two other members of the gang who are not identified. The men are dressed variously, some with a bulging white shirt such as Filch wears, and others in a military-style, knee-length coat like Macheath's. Some wear three-cornered hats; one of the unidentified members of the gang wears a patch over his left eye.

BEN: (*wiping his mouth on his sleeve after a long drink of wine*) But prithee, Matt, what is become of thy brother Tom? I have not seen him since my return from transportation.

MATT: Poor brother Tom had an accident this time twelve-month, and so clever a made fellow he was, that I could not save him from those flaying rascals the surgeons; and now, poor man, he is among the anatomies [1] at Surgeons' Hall.

BEN: (*sympathetically*) So, it seems, his time was come.

JEMMY: (*pounding the table forcefully*) But the present time is ours, and nobody alive hath more. Why are the laws levelled at us? Are we more dishonest than the rest of mankind? What we win, gentlemen, is our own by the law of arms and the right of conquest.

JACK: (*outspreading his arms and smiling*) Where shall we find such another set of practical philosophers, who to a man are above the fear of death?

WAT: (*without changing his melancholy expression*) Sound men, and true!

ROBIN: Of tried courage, and indefatigable industry!

NED: Who is there here who would not die for his friend?

HARRY: Who is there here that would betray him for his interest?

MATT: Show me a gang of courtiers that can say as much.

BEN: (*gleefully*) We are for a just partition of the world, for every man hath a right to enjoy life.

MATT: (*standing and orating*) <u>We re</u>trench the superfluities of mankind. The world is avaricious, and I hate avarice. A covetous fellow, like a jackdaw, steals what he was never made to enjoy, for the sake of hiding it. These are the robbers of mankind, for money was made for the free-hearted and generous; and where is the injury of taking from another, what he hath not the heart to make use of?

JEMMY: Our several stations for the day are fixed. Good luck attend us! Fill the glasses.

MATT: (*seating himself again, he begins to sing in a raucous bass*)

> *AIR XIX—Fill ev'ry glass, etc.*
> *Fill every glass, for wine inspires us,*
> 　　*And fires us,*
> *With courage, love, and joy.*
> *Women and wine should life employ.*
> *Is there aught else on earth desirous?*

OTHERS: (*in chorus*)

> *Fill every glass, for wine inspires us,*
> 　　*And fires us,*
> *With courage, love, and joy.*
> *Women and wine should life employ.*
> *Is there aught else on earth desirous?*

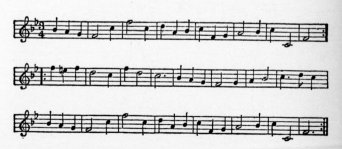

Scene Two

Macheath enters from the right as they finish the song. He raises his arm in a general greeting.

MACHEATH: (*boisterously*) Gentlemen, well met. My heart hath been with you this hour, but an unexpected affair hath detained me.

(*The men start to rise in honor of the captain, but he waves them down with his hand.*)

No ceremony, I beg you.

MATT: (*pleasantly*) We were just breaking up to go upon duty. Am I to have the honor of taking the air with you, sir, this evening upon the heath? I drink a dram now and then with the stage-coachmen in the way of friendship and intelligence, and I know that about this time there will be passengers upon the Western Road who are worth speaking with.

MACHEATH: (*hesitantly*) I was to have been of that party—but—

MATT: But what, sir?

MACHEATH: (*his voice suddenly crackling with authority*) Is there any man who suspects my courage?—

MATT: We have all been witnesses of it.—

MACHEATH: My honor and truth to the gang?

MATT: I'll be answerable for it.

MACHEATH: In the division of our booty, have I ever shown the least marks of avarice or injustice?

MATT: (*placatingly*) By these questions something seems to have ruffled you. Are any of us suspected?

MACHEATH: I have a fixed confidence, gentlemen, in you all, as men of honor, and as such I value and respect you. Peachum is a man that is useful to us.

MATT: (*grasping the butt of his pistol belligerently*) Is he about to play us any foul play? I'll shoot him through the head.

MACHEATH: (*coolly*) I beg you, gentlemen, act with conduct and discretion. A pistol is your last resort.

MATT: He knows nothing of this meeting.

MACHEATH: Business cannot go on without him. He is

a man who knows the world, and is a necessary agent to us.

(*His voice becomes lower and more confidential; the gang gathers closer.*)

We have had a slight difference, and till it is accommodated I shall be obliged to keep out of his way. Any private dispute of mine shall be of no ill consequence to my friends. You must continue to act under his direction, for the moment we break loose from him, our gang is ruined.

MATT: (*scratching his whiskers*) As a bawd to a whore, I grant you, he is to us of great convenience.

MACHEATH: Make him believe I have quitted the gang, which I can never do but with life. At our private quarters I will continue to meet you. A week or so will probably reconcile us.

MATT: (*tipping his hat in salute*) Your instructions shall be observed. 'Tis now high time for us to repair to our several duties; so till the evening at our quarters in Moor-fields we bid you farewell.

MACHEATH: (*sitting down melancholy at the table*) I shall wish myself with you. Success attend you.

MATT: (*singing to the men in a rousing bass voice*)

AIR XX—March in Rinaldo,[2] with drums and trumpets

> *Let us take the road.*
>> *Hark! I hear the sound of coaches!*
>> *The hour of attack approaches,*
> *To your arms, brave boys, and load.*

>> *See the ball I hold!*
> *Let the chymists toil like asses,*
> *Our fire their fire surpasses,*
>> *And turns all our lead to gold.*[3]

The gang, in a line at the front of the stage, load their pistols and stick them under their belts; then they go off-stage to the right, singing:

>> *Let us take the road.*
>>> *Hark! I hear the sound of coaches!*
>>> *The hour of attack approaches,*
>> *To your arms, brave boys, and load.*

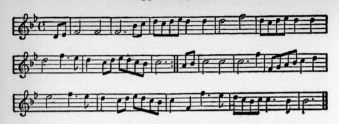

Scene Three

MACHEATH: (*his spirits reviving*) **What a fool is a fond wench!** Polly is most confoundedly bit—I love the sex. And a man who loves money might be as well contented with one guinea, as I with one woman. (*laughing at an amusing thought*) The town perhaps hath been as much obliged to me, for recruiting it with free-hearted ladies, as to any recruiting officer in the army. If it were not for us, and the other gentlemen of the sword, Drury Lane⁴ would be uninhabited. (*Sings, waving his tankard.*)

AIR XXI—Would you have a young virgin, etc.

>   *If the heart of a man is depressed with cares,*
>   *The mist is dispelled when a woman appears;*
>   *Like the notes of a fiddle, she sweetly, sweetly*
>   *Raises the spirits, and charms our ears.*
>   *Roses and lilies her cheeks disclose,*
>   *But her ripe lips are more sweet than those.*
>   *Press her, caress her*
>   *With blisses, her kisses*
>   *Dissolve us in pleasure and soft repose.*

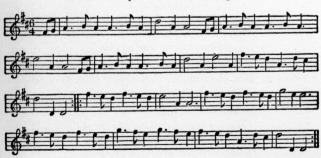

I must have women. There is nothing unbends the mind like them. Money is not so strong a cordial for the time. Drawer!—

(*The drawer, a slender little man wearing a brown periwig that is much too large for him and a white apron that almost touches the floor, rushes onstage from the right. His steps are so brisk and quick that he seems almost to be skipping.*)

Is the porter gone for all the ladies, according to my directions?

DRAWER: (*in a nervous, high-pitched voice*) I expect him back every minute. But you know, sir, you sent him as far as Hockley-in-the-Hole for three of the ladies, for one in Vinegar Yard, and for the rest of them somewhere about Lewkner's Lane.[5] (*There is the sound of a bell ringing off-stage.*) Sure some of them are below, for I hear the bar bell. As they come I will show them up. Coming! coming! (*He hurries off-stage to the right.*)

Scene Four

Macheath sees the eight women he has invited enter at the right, and he rises gallantly to greet them. At first glance these ladies of easy virtue seem hardly distinguishable from each other. All of them are carefully preened and coarsely pretty, and all of them are wearing clothes of the latest fashion. Each of the costumes is drawn tightly at the waist, with a square-cut, low neckline revealing large areas of powdered bosom. The dresses are worn over hoop petticoats and are versions of the then-popular Watteau sacque, *named after the artist who so often depicted it. All of the women wear round, puffed mobcaps (some tied like bonnets) with a feather at the top. In their actions they seem uniformly dedicated to mimicking the airs of high-born ladies. Mrs. Coaxer enters first and gives the captain a coy curtsy.*

MACHEATH: (*bowing*) Dear Mrs. Coaxer, you are welcome. You look charmingly to-day. (*She attempts a modest shrug of the shoulders.*) I hope you don't want the repairs of quality, and lay on paint.—Dolly Trull!

kiss me, you slut; are you as amorous as ever, hussy? (*Macheath moves to embrace her, but Dolly, whose innocent look contradicts her reputation, eludes him with mock prudishness.*) You are always so taken up with stealing hearts, that you don't allow yourself time to steal anything else. Ah Dolly, thou wilt ever be a coquette.—Mrs. Vixen, I'm yours! (*Mrs. Vixen, larger and plumper than the others, laughs heartily at Macheath's jest and busses him on the cheek.*) I always loved a woman of wit and spirit; they make charming mistresses, but plaguy wives.—Betty Doxy! come hither, hussy. Do you drink as hard as ever? (*Betty, whose puffy features and bleary eyes indicate that Macheath's remark has struck home, turns away in a huff.*) You had better stick to good, wholesome beer; for in troth, Betty, strong waters will, in time, ruin your constitution. You should leave those to your betters.—What! and my pretty Jenny Diver too! As prim and demure as ever! (*Jenny throws her head back and laughs uproariously; then she curtsies in mock innocence.*) There is not any prude, though ever so high bred, hath a more sanctified look, with a more mischievous heart. Ah! thou art a dear artful hypocrite!—Mrs. Slammekin! as careless and genteel as ever! (*He playfully tugs her dress down from her shoulder.*) all you fine ladies, who know your own beauty, affect an undress.—But see, here's Suky Tawdry come to contradict what I was saying. Everything she gets one way, she lays out upon her back. (*Suky glows at the compliment, not understanding Macheath's pun.*) Why Suky, you must keep at least a dozen tally-men.[6]—Molly Brazen! (*She kisses him full on the mouth.*) That's well done. I love a free-hearted wench. Thou hast a most agreeable assurance, girl, and art as willing as a turtle.[7]—But hark! I hear music. The harper is at the door. "If music be the food of love, play on." [8] Ere you seat yourselves, ladies, what think you of a dance? Come in. (*The harper, a short, fat man with bushy hair and a sad countenance, walks slowly in, carrying an instrument much like a modern zither.*)

Play the French tune that Mrs. Slammekin was so fond of. (*The harper strikes up his tune, and the group dances à la ronde in the French manner. Near the end of it Macheath begins singing, the ladies joining in on the chorus.*)

AIR XXII—Cotillion

> *Youth's the season made for joys,*
>> *Love is then our duty;*
> *She alone who that employs,*
>> *Well deserves her beauty.*
>>> *Let's be gay,*
>>> *While we may,*
> *Beauty's a flower despised in decay.*

CHORUS: *Youth's the season, etc.*

MACHEATH: *Let us drink and sport to-day,*
>> *Ours is not to-morrow.*
> *Love with youth flies swift away,*
>> *Age is nought but sorrow.*
>>> *Dance and sing,*
>>> *Time's on the wing,*
> *Life never knows the return of spring.*

CHORUS: *Let us drink, etc.*

MACHEATH: (*clapping his hands together*) Now pray, ladies, take your places. Here, fellow. (*He carelessly draws a banknote from his pocket and hands it to the harper without looking at the denomination.*) Bid the drawer bring us more wine. (*The harper tips his hat and goes out stage right.*)
If any of the ladies choose gin, I hope they will be so free to call for it.

JENNY: (*petulantly*) You look as if you meant me. Wine is strong enough for me. Indeed, sir, I never drink strong waters but when I have the colic.

MACHEATH: (*laughing heartily*) Just the excuse of the fine ladies! Why, a lady of quality is never without the colic. I hope, Mrs. Coaxer, you have had good success of late in your visits among the mercers.[9]

MRS. COAXER: (*obviously pleased to be discussing her profession*) We have so many interlopers. Yet, with industry, one may still have a little picking. I carried a sliver-flower lute-string and a piece of black padesoy [10] to Mr. Peachum's lock but last week.

MRS. VIXEN: (*enviously*) There's Molly Brazen hath the ogle [11] of a rattlesnake. She riveted a linen-draper's eye so fast upon her, that he was nicked of three pieces of cambric before he could look off.

MOLLY: (*spitefully*) Oh, dear madam! Be sure nothing can come up to your handling of laces! And then you have such a sweet deluding tongue! To cheat a man is nothing; but the woman must have fine parts indeed who cheats a woman!

MRS. VIXEN: (*cattily*) Lace, madam, lies in a small compass, and is of easy conveyance. But you are apt, madam, to think too well of your friends.

MRS. COAXER: (*archly*) If any woman hath more art than another, to be sure, 'tis Jenny Diver. Though her fellow be never so agreeable, she can pick his pocket as coolly as if money were her only pleasure. Now, that is a command of the passions uncommon in a woman!

JENNY: (*ruffled*) I never go to the tavern with a man but in the view of business. I have other hours, and other sort of men for my pleasure. But had I your address, madam—

MACHEATH: (*wearying of the ladies' bickering*) Have done with your compliments, ladies, and drink about. You are not so fond of me, Jenny, as you used to be.

JENNY: (*kittenishly*) 'Tis not convenient, sir, to show my kindness among so many rivals. 'Tis your own choice, and not the warmth of my inclination, that will determine you.

(*At this coquettish remark, Macheath laughs and pulls Jenny onto his lap. From this perch she begins to sing a saucy song.*)

AIR XXIII—All in a misty morning, etc.

Before the barn-door crowing,
  The cocks by hens attended,
His eyes around him throwing,
  Stands for a while suspended.
Then one he singles from the crew,
  And cheers the happy hen;
With "How do you do," and "How do you do,"
  And "How do you do" again.

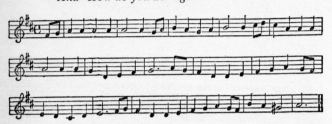

MACHEATH: (*nuzzling Jenny on the back of the neck*) Ah Jenny! thou art a dear slut.

DOLLY: (*to Suky Tawdry*) Pray, madam, were you ever in keeping?

SUKY: (*indignant*) I hope, madam, I han't been so long upon the town but I have met with some good fortune as well as my neighbors.

DOLLY: Pardon me, madam, I meant no harm by the question; 'twas only in the way of conversation.

SUKY: Indeed, madam, if I had not been a fool, I might have lived very handsomely with my last friend. But upon his missing five guineas, he turned me off. Now, I never suspected he had counted them.

MRS. SLAMMEKIN: (*to Dolly*) Who do you look upon, madam, as your best sort of keepers?

DOLLY: That, madam, is thereafter as they be.

MRS. SLAMMEKIN: I, madam, was once kept by a Jew; and bating their religion, to women they are a good sort of people.

SUKY: (*greedily*) Now for my part, I own I like an old fellow; for we always make them pay for what they can't do.

MRS. VIXEN: (*with enthusiasm*) A spruce prentice, let me tell you, ladies, is no ill thing; they bleed freely. I have sent at least two or three dozen of them in my time to the plantations.[12]

JENNY: (*caressing Macheath's shoulder*) But to be sure, sir, with so much good fortune as you have had upon the road, you must be grown immensely rich.

MACHEATH: The road, indeed, hath done me justice, but the gaming-table hath been my ruin.

JENNY: (*her arm about Macheath's waist*)

AIR XXIV—When once I lay with another man's wife, etc.
> *The gamesters and lawyers are jugglers alike,*
> *   If they meddle, your all is in danger:*
> *Like gypsies, if once they can finger a souse,[13]*
> *   Your pockets they pick, and they pilfer your house,*
> *And give your estate to a stranger.*

A man of courage should never put anything to the risque, but his life. These are the tools of a man of honor. Cards and dice are only fit for cowardly cheats, who prey upon their friends.

Macheath is so absorbed in Jenny's words that he does not notice that she has removed one of his pistols from his belt. Suky Tawdry, on the other side, relieves him of the other one.

SUKY: (*leveling the gun at his heart*) This, sir, is fitter for your hand. Besides your loss of money, 'tis a loss to the ladies. Gaming takes you off from women. How fond could I be of you!—but before company, 'tis ill bred.

MACHEATH: (*angry and hurt*) Wanton hussies!

JENNY: I must and will have a kiss, to give my wine a zest.

Jenny and Suky put their arms about Macheath's neck

and kiss him; then they make signs to Peachum and the constables, who are off-stage to the right, to come and apprehend the captain.

Scene Five

Peachum and two constables—dressed in military costumes with three-cornered hats—rush onto the stage. The constables seize Macheath while Peachum struts proudly around them.

PEACHUM: I seize you, sir, as my prisoner.

MACHEATH (*in tight-lipped fury*) Was this well done, Jenny? Women are decoy ducks: who can trust them? Beasts, jades, jilts, harpies, furies, whores!

PEACHUM: (*tauntingly*) Your case, Mr. Macheath, is not particular. The greatest heroes have been ruined by women. But, to do them justice, I must own they are a pretty sort of creatures, if we could trust them. You must now, sir, take your leave of the ladies, and if they have a mind to make you a visit, they will be sure to find you at home. The gentleman, ladies, lodges in Newgate. Constables, wait upon the captain to his lodgings.

MACHEATH: (*bitterly*)

AIR XXV—When first I laid siege to my Chloris, etc.
> *At the tree I shall suffer with pleasure,*
> *At the tree I shall suffer with pleasure;*
>   *Let me go where I will,*
>   *In all kinds of ill,*
> *I shall find no such furies as these are.*

PEACHUM: Ladies, I'll take care the reckoning shall be discharged.

Macheath, closely guarded by the two constables,

leaves the stage to the right, with Peachum following.
Macheath looks back at the ladies and scowls.

Scene Six

MRS. VIXEN: (*avariciously*) Look ye, Mrs. Jenny;
though Mr. Peachum may have made a private bargain
with you and Suky Tawdry for betraying the captain, as
we were all assisting, we ought to share alike.

MRS. COAXER: (*green with envy*) I think Mr. Peachum,
after so long an acquaintance, might have trusted me as
well as Jenny Diver.

MRS. SLAMMEKIN: (*boastfully*) I am sure at least
three men of his hanging, and in a year's time too, (if he
did me justice) should be set down to my account.

DOLLY: (*indignantly*) Mrs. Slammekin, that is not
fair. For you know one of them was taken in bed
with me.

JENNY: (*dismissing the subject*) As far as a bowl of
punch or a treat, I believe Mrs. Suky will join with me.
As for anything else, ladies, you cannot in conscience expect it.

The ladies prepare to go out at the right, but become
involved in an Alphonse-Gaston predicament. Each lady
curtsies grandly, mimicking the ladies of quality, and
insists that the other precede her through the doorway.

MRS. SLAMMEKIN: Dear madam—

DOLLY: I would not for the world—

MRS. SLAMMEKIN: 'Tis impossible for me—

DOLLY: As I hope to be saved, madam—

MRS. SLAMMEKIN: Nay, then I must stay here all
night.—

DOLLY: Since you command me.

Dolly goes out, and the rest follow.

Scene Seven

The scene is Newgate Prison a few minutes later. Mac-
heath is outside a cell with Lockit, the turnkey at New-
gate. Lockit is a stocky man, slightly below medium
height. His appearance is far from neat; he wears sev-

*eral days' growth of whiskers, and his stockings have
become unfastened and have gathered about his calves
in wrinkles. His three-quarter-length coat, once a handsome garment, is only partially buttoned, revealing the
fact that he wears no shirt beneath it. He has a soft,
peaked hat plumped carelessly on his head. His ready
smile shows immediately that despite his profession he is
a man of merry spirits. Macheath has by now recovered
his customary aplomb. Hanging on the wall outside the
cell are a number of wrist irons which are used to fetter
the prisoners.*

LOCKIT: (*cordially*) Noble captain, you are welcome.
You have not been a lodger of mine this year and half.
You know the custom, sir. Garnish, captain, garnish! [14]
(*He points to some irons hanging high on the wall.*)
Hand me down those fetters there.

MACHEATH: (*shaking his head*) Those, Mr. Lockit,
seem to be the heaviest of the whole set! With your leave,
I should like the further pair better.

LOCKIT: Look ye, captain, we know what is fittest for
our prisoners. When a gentleman uses me with civility, I
always do the best I can to please him.—Hand them
down, I say.—We have them of all prices, from one
guinea to ten, and 'tis fitting every gentleman should
please himself.
(*He peers closely at Macheath to determine whether or
not the captain understands his threat.*)

MACHEATH: I understand you, sir. (*He takes a banknote from his pocket and hands it to Lockit.*) The fees
here are so many, and so exorbitant, that few fortunes
can bear the expense of getting off handsomely, or of dying like a gentleman.

LOCKIT: (*enjoying Macheath's clever rebuke*) Those,
I see, will fit the captain better. Take down the further
pair. Do but examine them, sir,—never was better work.
How genteelly they are made! They will fit as easy as a
glove, and the nicest man in England might not be
ashamed to wear them. (*He puts on the chains and mo-*

tions Macheath into the cell.) If I had the best gentleman in the land in my custody, I could not equip him more handsomely. And so, sir—I now leave you to your private meditations.

Scene Eight

Macheath, his wrists in chains, looks out through the bars and begins to sing.

MACHEATH:

AIR XXVI—Courtiers, courtiers, think it no harm, etc.
> *Man may escape from rope and gun;*
> *Nay, some have outlived the doctor's pill;*
> *Who takes a woman must be undone,*
>   *That basilisk is sure to kill.*
>
> *The fly that sips treacle is lost in the sweets,*
> *So he that tastes woman, woman, woman,*
>   *He that tastes woman, ruin meets.*

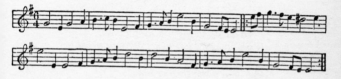

To what a woeful plight have I brought myself! Here must I (all day long till I'm hanged) be confined to hear the reproaches of a wench who lays her ruin at my door. I am in the custody of her father, and to be sure if he knows of the matter, I shall have a fine time on't betwixt this and my execution. But I promised the wench marriage. What signifies a promise to a woman? Does not a man in marriage itself promise a hundred things that he never means to perform? Do all we can, women will believe us; for they look upon a promise as an excuse for following their own inclinations.—But here comes Lucy, and I cannot get from her. Would I were deaf! (*He places his hands over his ears; the chains dangle beneath his chin.*)

Scene Nine

Lucy Lockit, who is the counterpart of Polly Peachum in the play, enters from the right. She is coarsely pretty, with raven hair and sparkling black eyes. Her lime-green dress, which is a Watteau sacque *cut in the latest fashion, is pulled low, exposing most of her bosom. She wears her dress short, revealing several inches of lace petticoat and a pair of trim ankles. A close observer would note that she is in the early stages of pregnancy. She is irate, and her anger has reddened her face, heightening the beauty of this high-spirited wench.*

LUCY: You base man, you, how can you look me in the face after what has passed between us?—See here, perfidious wretch, how I am forced to bear about the load of infamy you have laid upon me—O Macheath! thou hast robbed me of my quiet—to see thee tortured would give me pleasure.

> *AIR XXVII—A lovely lass to a friar came, etc.*
> *Thus when a good housewife sees a rat*
> *In a trap in the morning taken,*
> *With pleasure her heart goes pit-a-pat*
> *In revenge for her loss of bacon.*
> *Then she throws him*
> *To the dog or cat*
> *To be worried, crushed, and shaken.*

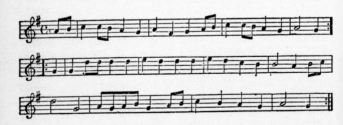

MACHEATH: (*making a great show at appearing wounded*) Have you no bowels, no tenderness, my dear Lucy, to see a husband in these circumstances?

LUCY: A husband!

MACHEATH: (*gallantly*) In every respect but the form, and that, my dear, may be said over us at any time. Friends should not insist upon ceremonies. From a man of honor, his word is as good as his bond.

LUCY: (*unconvinced*) 'Tis the pleasure of all you fine men to insult the women you have ruined.

AIR XXVIII—'Twas when the sea was roaring, etc.

> How cruel are the traitors
>   Who lie and swear in jest,
> To cheat unguarded creatures
>   Of virtue, fame, and rest!
>
> Whoever steals a shilling
>   Through shame the guilt conceals;
> In love, the perjured villain
>   With boasts the theft reveals.

MACHEATH: (*soothingly*) The very first opportunity may dear, (have but patience) you shall be my wife in whatever manner you please.

LUCY: (*furiously*) Insinuating monster! And so you think I know nothing of the affair of Miss Polly Peachum. I could tear thy eyes out!

MACHEATH: (*attempting bravado*) Sure, Lucy, you can't be such a fool as to be jealous of Polly!

LUCY: (*rattling the bars as if attempting to break them down*) Are you not married to her, you brute, you?

MACHEATH: (*improvising quickly*) Married! Very good. The wench gives it out only to vex thee, and to ruin me in thy good opinion. 'Tis true I go to the house; I chat with the girl, I kiss her, I say a thousand things to her (as all gentlemen do) that mean nothing, to divert myself; and now the silly jade hath set it about that I am married to her, to let me know what she would be at. Indeed, my dear Lucy, these violent passions may be of ill consequence to a woman in your condition.

LUCY: (*warming slightly*) Come, come, captain, for all your assurance, you know that Miss Polly hath put it out of your power to do me the justice you promised me.

MACHEATH: (*reaching from behind the bars to caress her cheek*) A jealous woman believes everything her passion suggests. To convince you of my sincerity, if we can find the ordinary,[15] I shall have no scruples of making you my wife—and I know the consequence of having two at a time.

LUCY: (*outwitting him*) That you are only to be hanged, and so get rid of them both.

MACHEATH: (*benignly*) I am ready, my dear Lucy, to give you satisfaction—if you think there is any in marriage. What can a man of honor say more?

LUCY: (*convinced at last*) So then it seems—you are not married to Miss Polly.

MACHEATH: (*confidently*) You know, Lucy, the girl is prodigiously conceited. No man can say a civil thing to her, but (like other fine ladies) her vanity makes her think he's her own for ever and ever.

AIR XXIX—The sun had loosed his weary teams, etc.

> *The first time at the looking-glass*
> > *The mother sets her daughter,*
> *The image strikes the smiling lass*
> > *With self-love ever after.*
> *Each time she looks, she, fonder grown,*
> > *Thinks every charm grows stronger.*
> *But alas, vain maid, all eyes but your own*
> > *Can see you are not younger.*

When women consider their own beauties, they are all alike unreasonable in their demands; for they expect their lovers should like them as long as they like themselves.

LUCY: Yonder is my father. Perhaps this way we may light upon the ordinary, who shall try if you will be as good as your word; for I long to be made an honest woman. (*She rushes out excitedly.*)

Scene Ten

The scene is Lockit's room at Newgate Prison, immediately following the previous action. The room is as disorderly as Lockit himself; clothing is strewed about on the floor and on the bed. On a small table is a collection of broken wrist irons and chains. Peachum and Lockit are seated on the bed, studying Lockit's account-book.

LOCKIT: In this last affair, brother Peachum, we are agreed. You have consented to go halves in Macheath.

PEACHUM: (*shrugging*) We shall never fall out about an execution. But as to that article, pray how stands our last year's account?

LOCKIT: (*proudly*) If you will run your eye over it, you'll find 'tis fair and clearly stated.

PEACHUM: This long arrear[16] of the government is very hard upon us! Can it be expected that we should hang our acquaintance for nothing, when our betters will hardly save theirs without being paid for it? Unless the people in employment[17] pay better, I promise them for the future, I shall let other rogues live besides their own.

LOCKIT: Perhaps, brother, they are afraid these matters may be carried too far. We are treated, too, by them with contempt, as if our profession were not reputable.

PEACHUM: (*boldly*) In one respect, indeed, our employment may be reckoned dishonest, because, like great statesmen, we encourage those who betray their friends.

LOCKIT: (*fearfully*) Such language, brother, anywhere else might turn to your prejudice. Learn to be more guarded, I beg you.

> *AIR XXX*—How happy are we, etc.
> *When you censure the age,*
> *Be cautious and sage,*
> Lest the courtiers offended should be.
> *If you mention vice or bribe,*
> *'Tis so pat to all the tribe*
> Each cries—That was levelled at me.

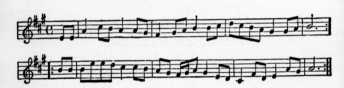

PEACHUM: (*returning to the account book*) Here's poor Ned Clincher's name, I see. Sure, brother Lockit, there was a little unfair proceeding in Ned's case; for he told me in the condemned hold, that for value received, you had promised him a session or two longer without molestation.

LOCKIT: (*incensed*) Mr. Peachum, this is the first time my honor was ever called in question.

PEACHUM: (*pompously*) Business is at an end, if once we act dishonorably.

LOCKIT: Who accuses me?

PEACHUM: You are warm, brother.

LOCKIT: He that attacks my honor, attacks my livelihood. And this usage, sir, is not to be borne.

PEACHUM: Since you provoke me to speak, I must tell you too, that Mrs. Coaxer charges you with defrauding her of her information-money, for the apprehending of curl-pated Hugh. Indeed, indeed, brother, we must punctually pay our spies, or we shall have no information.

LOCKIT: (*suddenly very angry*) Is this language to me, sirrah? Who have saved you from the gallows, sirrah!

They collar each other and begin to wrestle awkwardly.

PEACHUM: (*out of breath*) If I am hanged, it shall be for ridding the world of an arrant rascal.

LOCKIT: (*also laboring for breath*) This hand shall do the office of the halter you deserve, and throttle you, you dog!

They break apart.

PEACHUM:—Brother, brother,—we are both losers in the dispute—for you know we have it in our power to hang each other. You should not be so passionate.

LOCKIT: (*brushing off his clothes*) Nor you so provoking.

PEACHUM: 'Tis our mutual interest, 'tis for the interest of the world, we should agree. If I said anything, brother, to the prejudice of your character, I ask pardon.

LOCKIT: Brother Peachum, I can forgive as well as resent.—Give me your hand. Suspicion does not become a friend.

PEACHUM: I only meant to give you occasion to justify yourself. But I must now step home, for I expect the gentleman about this snuff-box that Filch nimmed two nights ago in the park. I appointed him at this hour. (*Peachum goes out, stage right.*)

Scene Eleven

Lucy enters from the left, weeping.

LOCKIT: (*roughly*) Whence come you, hussy?

LUCY: My tears might answer that question.

LOCKIT: You have been whimpering and fondling, like a spaniel, over the fellow that hath abused you.

LUCY: (*wiping the tears from her eyes daintily*) One can't help love; one can't cure it. 'Tis not in my power to obey you, and hate him.

LOCKIT: Learn to bear your husband's death like a reasonable woman. 'Tis not the fashion, nowadays, so much as to affect sorrow upon these occasions. No woman would ever marry if she had not the chance of mortality for release. Act like a woman of spirit, hussy, and thank your father for what he is doing.

LUCY:

AIR XXXI—Of a noble race was Shenkin.

> *Is then his fate decreed, sir?*
> *Such a man can I think of quitting?*
> *When first we met, so moves me yet,*
> *Oh, see how my heart is splitting!*

LOCKIT: (*somewhat sympathetically*) Look ye, Lucy—there is no saving him—so, I think, you must even do like other widows,—buy yourself weeds, and be cheerful.

AIR XXXII

> *You'll think, ere many days ensue,*
> *This sentence not severe;*
> *I hang your husband, child, 'tis true,*
> *But with him hang your care.*
> *Twang dang dillo dee.*

Like a good wife, go moan over your dying husband; that, child, is your duty.—Consider, girl, you can't have the man and the money too—so make yourself as easy as you can by getting all you can from him. (*They go out, stage right.*)

Scene Twelve

The scene is Macheath's cell, in another part of the prison, a few minutes later. Lucy is talking with the captain through the bars.

LUCY: Though the ordinary was out of the way today, I hope, my dear, you will, upon the first opportunity, quiet my scruples.—Oh, sir!—my father's hard heart is not to be softened, and I am in the utmost despair. (*She drops her head on her breast in dejection.*)

MACHEATH: (*toying with a button on Lucy's bodice*) But if I could raise a small sum—would not twenty guineas, think you, move him?—Of all the arguments in the way of business, the perquisite is the most prevailing.—Your father's perquisites for the escape of prisoners must amount to a considerable sum in the year. Money well timed and properly applied will do anything.

AIR XXXIII—London ladies.

If you at an office solicit your due,
  And would not have matters neglected;
You must quicken the clerk with the perquisite too,
  To do what his duty directed.
Or would you the frowns of a lady prevent,
  She too has this palpable failing,
The perquisite softens her into consent;
  That reason with all is prevailing.

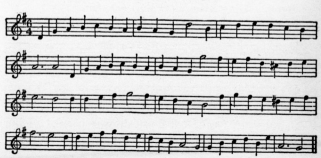

LUCY: (*a glimmer of hope in her eyes*) What love or money can do shall be done, for all my comfort depends upon your safety.

Scene Thirteen

Polly hurries onstage from the left. She is a picture of distress and anxiety.

POLLY: Where is my dear husband?—Was a rope ever intended for this neck?—Oh, let me throw my arms about it, and throttle thee with love! (*Polly reaches through the bars to embrace him, but Macheath retreats, covering his face in despair.*)—Why dost thou turn away from me?—'Tis thy Polly—'tis thy wife.

MACHEATH: Was there ever such an unfortunate rascal as I am!

LUCY: (*shouting angrily*) Was there ever such another villain!

POLLY: (*so distraught she is unaware of Lucy's presence*) O Macheath! was it for this we parted? Taken! imprisoned! tried! hanged!—cruel reflection! I'll stay with thee till death—no force shall tear thy dear wife from thee now.—What means my love?—not one kind word!—not one kind look! Think what thy Polly suffers to see thee in this condition.

AIR XXXIV—All in the downs, etc.
Thus when the swallow, seeking prey,
    Within the sash is closely pent,
His consort, with bemoaning lay,
    Without, sits pining for the event.
Her chattering lovers all around her skim;
    She heeds them not (poor bird)—her soul's with him.

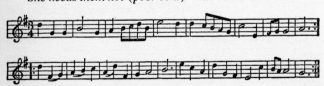

MACHEATH: (*aside*) I must disown her.—(*turning to Lucy*) The wench is distracted.

LUCY: (*refusing to be taken in*) Am I then bilked of my virtue? Can I have no reparation? Sure, men were born to lie, and women to believe them. (*furiously*) O villain! villain!

POLLY: (*fearing the worst*) Am I not thy wife? Thy neglect of me, thy aversion to me, too severely proves it. —Look on me. Tell me; am I not thy wife?

LUCY: Perfidious wretch!

POLLY: Barbarous husband!

LUCY: Hadst thou been hanged five months ago, I had been happy.

POLLY: And I too. If you had been kind to me till death, it would not have vexed me—and that's no very unreasonable request (though from a wife) to a man who hath not above seven or eight days to live.

LUCY: (*raging*) Art thou then married to another? Hast thou two wives, monster?

MACHEATH: If women's tongues can cease for an answer—hear me.

LUCY: I won't! Flesh and blood can't bear my usage.

POLLY: Shall I not claim my own? Justice bids me speak.

MACHEATH:

AIR XXXV—Have you heard of a frolicsome ditty, etc.
> *How happy I could be with either,*
> *Were t'other dear charmer away!*
> *But while you thus tease me together,*
> *To neither a word will I say;*
> *But tol de rol, etc.*

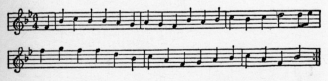

POLLY: (*naively*) Sure, my dear, there ought to be some preference shown to a wife! At least she may claim the appearance of it.—He must be distracted with his misfortunes, or he could not use me thus!

LUCY: O villain, villain! thou hast deceived me—I could even inform against thee with pleasure. Not a prude wishes more heartily to have facts against her intimate acquaintance, than I now wish to have facts against thee. I would have her satisfaction, and they should all out.

AIR XXXVI—Irish Trot.

POLLY: I'm bubbled.[18]

LUCY: —I'm bubbled!

POLLY: Oh how I am troubled!

LUCY: Bamboozled, and bit!

POLLY: —My distresses are doubled.

LUCY: When you come to the tree, should the hang-
        man refuse,
        These fingers, with pleasure, could fasten the
        noose.

POLLY: (*beginning the duet again*) I'm bubbled, etc.

MACHEATH: (*reaching through the bars for Lucy, who backs away from him*) Be pacified, my dear Lucy! —This is all a fetch of Polly's to make me desperate with you in case I get off. If I am hanged, she would fain have the credit of being thought my widow. (*turning to Polly, sternly*)—Really, Polly, this is no time for a dispute of this sort; for whenever you are talking of marriage, I am thinking of hanging.

POLLY: (*tearfully*) And hast thou the heart to persist in disowning me?

MACHEATH: And hast thou the heart to persist in

persuading me that I am married? Why, Polly, dost
thou seek to aggravate my misfortunes?

LUCY: *Really*, Miss Peachum, you but expose yourself. Besides, 'tis barbarous in you to worry a gentleman
in his circumstances.

POLLY:

AIR XXXVII

Cease your funning,
  Force or cunning
Never shall my heart trepan.[19]
  All these sallies
  Are but malice
To seduce my constant man.

  'Tis most certain,
  By their flirting,
Women oft have envy shown;
  Pleased to ruin
  Other's wooing;
Never happy in their own!

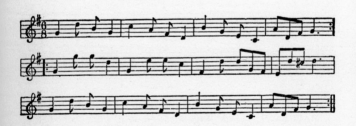

LUCY: (*haughtily*) Decency, madam, methinks, might
teach you to behave yourself with some reserve with the
husband while his wife is present.

MACHEATH: But, seriously, Polly, this is carrying
the joke a little too far.

LUCY: If you are determined, madam, to raise a
disturbance in the prison, I shall be obliged to send for
the turnkey to show you the door. I am sorry, madam,
you force me to be so ill-bred.

POLLY: (*sarcastically, with undue emphasis on the word* madam) Give me leave to tell you, madam; these forward airs don't become you in the least, madam. And my duty, madam, obliges me to stay with my husband, madam.

LUCY:

AIR XXXVIII—Good-morrow, gossip Joan.
> *Why, how now, Madam Flirt?*
> *If you thus must chatter;*
> *And are for flinging dirt,*
>   *Let's try who best can spatter!*
>   *Madam Flirt!*

POLLY:	*Why, how now, saucy jade;*
	Sure the wench is tipsy!
(*to Macheath*)	*How can you see me made*
	The scoff of such a gipsy?
(*to Lucy*)	*Saucy jade!*

Scene Fourteen

Peachum enters angrily from the right. He is a perfect parody of the outraged father.

PEACHUM: Where's my wench? Ah hussy! hussy!—Come you home, you slut; and when your fellow is hanged, hang yourself, to make your family some amends.

POLLY: Dear, dear father, do not tear me from him! I must speak; I have more to say to him. (*reaching through the bars imploringly to Macheath*) Oh! twist thy fetters about me, that he may not haul me from thee!

PEACHUM: (*irascibly*) Sure, all women are alike! If ever they commit the folly, thèy are sure to commit another by exposing themselves.—Away—not a word more—you are my prisoner now, hussy!
(*He grasps Polly roughly.*)

POLLY: (*desperately holding onto Macheath while Peachum tries to pull her away*)

AIR XXXIX—Irish howl.
No power on earth can e'er divide
The knot that sacred love hath tied.
When parents draw against our mind,
The true-love's knot they faster bind.
    Oh, oh ray, oh amborah—Oh, oh, etc.

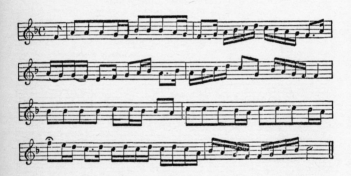

With a mighty tug, Peachum pulls Polly away from Macheath and forces her, still struggling, to go out, stage right.

Scene Fifteen

MACHEATH: (*using all his charms to convince Lucy of his sincerity*) I am naturally compassionate, wife, so that I could not use the wench as she deserved, which made you at first suspect there was something in what she said.

LUCY: Indeed, my dear, I was strangely puzzled.

MACHEATH: If that had been the case, her father would never have brought me into this circumstance. No, Lucy,—I had rather die than be false to thee.

LUCY: How happy am I if you say this from your heart! For I love thee so, that I could sooner bear to see thee hanged than in the arms of another.

MACHEATH: But couldst thou bear to see me hanged?

LUCY: (*horror-stricken*) O Macheath, I can never live to see that day.

MACHEATH: (*coming to the main point in his argument*) You see, Lucy; in the account of love you are in my debt, and you must now be convinced that I rather choose to die than to be another's. Make me, if possible, love thee more, and let me owe my life to thee. If you refuse to assist me, Peachum and your father will immediately put me beyond all means of escape.

LUCY: (*her eyes lighting up*) My father, I know, hath been drinking hard with the prisoners, and I fancy he is now taking his nap in his own room. If I can procure the keys, shall I go off with thee, my dear?

MACHEATH: (*thinking quickly*) If we are together, 'twill be impossible to lie concealed. As soon as the search begins to be a little cool, I will send to thee— till then, my heart is thy prisoner.

LUCY: Come then, my dear husband—owe thy life to me—and though you love me not—be grateful. But that Polly runs in my head strangely.

MACHEATH: (*impatient, but still trying to be charming*) A moment of time may make us unhappy forever.

LUCY:

> *AIR XL*—The lass of Patie's mill, etc.
>   *I like the fox shall grieve,*
>   *Whose mate hath left her side,*
>   *Whom hounds, from morn till eve,*
>   *Chase o'er the country wide,*
>   *Where can my lover hide?*
>   *Where cheat the wary pack?*
>   *If love be not his guide,*
>   *He never will come back!*

End of the second Act

*She goes out to the right, pausing at the door to
blow a kiss back to Macheath in the cell.*

ACT III

Scene One

The scene is Lockit's room at Newgate Prison, perhaps an hour later. The room is as disorderly as before. Lockit is enraged, pacing the floor and shouting at Lucy, who is kneeling.

LOCKIT: To be sure, wench, you must have been aiding and abetting to help him to this escape.

LUCY: Sir, here hath been Peachum and his daughter Polly, and to be sure they know the ways of Newgate as well as if they had been born and bred in the place all their lives. Why must all your suspicion light upon me?

LOCKIT: (*drawing back his arm as if to strike her*) Lucy, Lucy, I will have none of these shuffling answers.

LUCY: (*showing her spirit*) Well then—if I know anything of him, I wish I may be burnt!

LOCKIT: Keep your temper, Lucy, or I shall pronounce you guilty.

LUCY: (*rising to her feet*) Keep yours, sir. I do wish I may be burnt, I do. And what can I say more to convince you?

LOCKIT: Did he tip handsomely? How much did he come down with? (*showing his greed*) Come, hussy, don't cheat your father, and I shall not be angry with you. Perhaps you have made a better bargain with him than I could have done. How much, my good girl?

LUCY: You know, sir, I am fond of him, and would have given money to have kept him with me.

LOCKIT: (*clapping his forehead*) Ah, Lucy! thy education might have put thee more upon thy guard; for a girl in the bar of an ale-house is always besieged.

LUCY: (*sadly*) Dear sir, mention not my education —for 'twas to that I owe my ruin.

> *AIR XLI—If love's a sweet passion, etc.*
> *When young, at the bar you first taught me to score,*
> *And bid me be free of my lips, and no more.*
> *I was kissed by the parson, the squire, and the sot;*
> *When the guest was departed, the kiss was forgot.*
> *But his kiss was so sweet, and so closely he prest,*
> *That I languished and pined till I granted the rest.*

If you can forgive me, sir, I will make a fair confession, for to be sure he hath been a most barbarous villain to me.

LOCKIT: And so you have let him escape, hussy, have you?

LUCY: (*starry-eyed*) When a woman loves, a kind look, a tender word can persuade her to anything,— and I could ask no other bribe.

LOCKIT: Thou wilt always be a vulgar slut, Lucy.

If you would not be looked upon as a fool, you should never do anything but upon the foot of interest. Those that act otherwise are their own bubbles.[1]

LUCY: (*philosophically*) But love, sir, is a misfortune that may happen to the most discreet woman, and in love we are all fools alike. (*showing a trace of bitterness*) Not withstanding all he swore, I am now fully convinced that Polly Peachum is actually his wife. Did I let him escape (fool that I was) to go to her? Polly will wheedle herself into his money, and then Peachum will hang him, and cheat us both.

LOCKIT: So I am to be ruined, because, forsooth, you must be in love!—a very pretty excuse!

LUCY: (*giving full vent to her anger*) I could murder that impudent happy strumpet! I gave him his life, and that creature enjoys the sweets of it. Ungrateful Macheath!

AIR XLII—South-sea Ballad

My love is all madness and folly,
   Alone I lie,
   Toss, tumble, and cry;
What a happy creature is Polly!
Was e'er such a wretch as I!
With rage I redden like scarlet,
That my dear, inconstant varlet,
   Stark blind to my charms,
   Is lost in the arms   } *bis*
Of that jilt, that inveigling harlot!
This, this my resentment alarms.

LOCKIT: And so, after all this mischief, I must stay here to be entertained with your caterwauling, mistress Puss! (*He flails at her in his anger.*) Out of my sight, wanton strumpet! You shall fast and fortify yourself into reason, with now and then a little handsome discipline to bring you to your senses. Go!

(*He strikes at her again, and Lucy scrambles out of his reach and goes out stage right.*)

Scene Two

LOCKIT: (*pacing the stage nervously as he soliloquizes*)—Peachum then intends to outwit me in this affair, but I'll be even with him. The dog is leaky in his liquor; so I'll ply him that way, get the secret from him, and turn this affair to my own advantage. Lions, wolves, and vultures don't live together in herds, droves, or flocks. Of all animals of prey, man is the only sociable one. Every one of us preys upon his neighbor, and yet we herd together. Peachum is my companion, my friend. According to the custom of the world, indeed, he may quote thousands of precedents for cheating me. And shall I not make use of the privilege of friendship to make him a return?

AIR XLIII—Packington's Pound

Thus gamesters united in friendship are found,
Though they know, that their industry all is a cheat;
They flock to their prey at the dice-box's sound,
And join to promote one another's deceit.
*   But if by mishap*
*   They fail of a chap.*
To keep in their hands, they each other entrap.
Like pikes, lank with hunger, who miss of their ends,
They bite their companions, and prey on their friends.

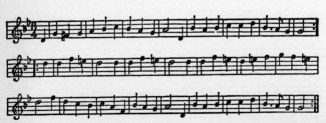

Now, Peachum, you and I, like honest tradesmen, are to have a fair trial which of us two can over-reach the other. (*calling loudly*) Lucy!

(*Lucy enters at the right.*)

Are there any of Peachum's people now in the house?

LUCY: Filch, sir, is drinking a quartern of strong waters in the next room with Black Moll.

LOCKIT: Bid him come to me.

Lucy hurries obediently off to the right.

Scene Three

Filch walks slowly on stage from the right, looking more slovenly and lackadaisical than usual.

LOCKIT: (*heartily*) Why, boy, thou lookest as if thou wert half starved—like a shotten herring.[2]

FILCH: (*wearily*) One had need have the constitution of a horse to go through the business. Since the favorite child-getter was disabled by mishap, I have picked up a little money by helping the ladies to a pregnancy against their being called down to sentence. But if a man cannot get an honest livelihood any easier way, I am sure 'tis what I can't undertake for another session.

LOCKIT: (*reflectively*) Truly, if that great man should tip off, 'twould be an irreparable loss. The vigor and prowess of a knight-errant never saved half of the ladies in distress that he hath done.—But, boy, canst thou tell me where thy master is to be found?

FILCH: At his lock, sir, at the Crooked Billet.

LOCKIT: Very well. I have nothing more with you. (*He gestures summarily, and Filch ambles off to the right.*) I'll go to him there, for I have many important affairs to settle with him; and in the way of those transactions, I'll artfully get into his secret, so that Macheath shall not remain a day longer out o' my clutches.

Scene Four

The scene is a gaming-house, immediately following the previous action. Macheath, dressed in a fine tarnished coat, is seated at a table with Ben Budge and Matt of the Mint, both dressed as before. The game

*of cards has just been concluded, and Macheath is
settling his debts. Behind them there are other men
seated at tables, playing cards or turning the dice-boxes.*

MACHEATH: (*cheerfully*) I am sorry, gentlemen, the
road was so barren of money. When my friends are in
difficulties, I am always glad that my fortune can be
serviceable to them. (*He tosses the bank-notes onto the
table with a grand and careless gesture.*) You see,
gentlemen, I am not a mere court friend, who professes
everything and will do nothing.

AIR XLIV—Lillibullero
*The modes of the court so common are grown,
    That a true friend can hardly be met;
Friendship for interest is but a loan,
    Which they let out for what they can get.
        'Tis true, you find
        Some friends so kind,
Who will give you good counsel themselves to defend.
        In sorrowful ditty,
        They promise, they pity,
But shift you, for money, from friend to friend.*

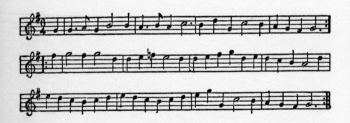

But we, gentlemen, have still honor enough to break
through the corruptions of the world. And while I can
serve you, you may command me.

BEN: (*shaking his head in genuine sadness*) It grieves
my heart that so generous a man should be involved in
such difficulties as oblige him to live with such ill company, and herd with gamesters.

MATT: (*in his cups and speaking louder than necessary*) See the partiality of mankind! One man may steal

a horse, better than another look over a hedge. Of all mechanics, of all servile handicrafts-men, a gamester is the vilest. But yet, as many of the quality are of the profession, he is admitted amongst the politest company. I wonder we are not more respected.

MACHEATH: (*returning quickly to matters of business*) There will be deep play tonight at Marybone and consequently money may be picked up upon the road. Meet me there, and I'll give you the hint who is worth setting.[3]

MATT: (*gesturing secretively at one of the players*) The fellow with a brown coat with a narrow gold binding, I am told, is never without money.

MACHEATH: What do you mean, Matt? Sure you will not think of meddling with him! He's a good honest kind of a fellow, and one of us.

BEN: To be sure, sir, we will put ourselves under your direction.

MACHEATH: Have an eye upon the money-lenders. A rouleau[4] or two would prove a pretty sort of an expedition. I hate extortion.

MATT: These rouleaus are very pretty things. I hate your bank bills. There is such a hazard in putting them off.

MACHEATH: (*confidentially*) There is a certain man of distinction who in his time hath nicked me out of a great deal of the ready. He is in my cash, Ben. I'll point him out to you this evening, and you shall draw upon him for the debt.—The company are met; I hear the dice-box in the other room. (*He rises to his feet gallantly.*) So, gentlemen, your servant! You'll meet me at Marybone. (*He hurries out to the left.*)

Scene Five

The scene is Peachum's lock, about three hours later. Peachum and Lockit are imbibing freely from the bottles of wine and brandy on the table in front of them. Lockit is smoking a pipe as he looks over the account book.

LOCKIT: The Coronation account,[5] brother Peachum,

is of so intricate a nature, that I believe it will never be settled.

PEACHUM: (*agreeably*) It consists, indeed, of a great variety of articles. It was worth to our people, in fees of different kinds, above ten installments. This is part of the account, brother, that lies open before us.

LOCKIT: (*pursing his lips thoughtfully*) A lady's tail [6] of rich brocade—that, I see, is disposed of—

PEACHUM: To Mrs. Diana Trapes, the tallywoman, and she will make a good hand on't in shoes and slippers, to trick out young ladies upon their going into keeping.

LOCKIT: (*puzzled*) But I don't see any article of the jewels.

PEACHUM: (*somewhat flustered*) Those are so well known that they must be sent abroad. You'll find them entered under the article of exportation. As for the snuff-boxes, watches, swords, etc., I thought it best to enter them under their several heads.

LOCKIT: Seven and twenty women's pockets complete, with the several things therein contained—all sealed, numbered, and entered.

PEACHUM: But, brother, it is impossible for us now to enter upon this affair.—We should have the whole day before us.—Besides, the account of the last half-year's plate is in a book by itself, which lies at the other office.

LOCKIT: (*jovially*) Bring us then more liquor.—To-day shall be for pleasure—tomorrow for business.—Ah, brother, those daughters of ours are two slippery hussies. Keep a watchful eye upon Polly, and Macheath in a day or two shall be our own again.

> *AIR XLV—Down in the North Country, etc.*
>> *What gudgeons [7] are we men!*
>>> *Every woman's easy prey;*
>> *Though we have felt the hook, again*
>>> *We bite and they betray.*
>> *The bird that hath been trapped,*
>>> *When he hears his calling mate,*
>> *To her he flies, again he's clapped*
>>> *Within the wiry grate.*

PEACHUM: (*tartly*) But what signifies catching the bird if your daughter Lucy will set open the door of the cage?

LOCKIT: (*shrugging his shoulders*) If men were answerable for the follies and frailities of their wives and daughters, no friends could keep a good correspondence together for two days.—This is unkind of you, brother, for among good friends, what they say or do goes for nothing.

(*A servant enters from the right.*)

SERVANT: Sir, here's Mrs. Diana Trapes wants to speak with you.

PEACHUM: Shall we admit her, brother Lockit?

LOCKIT: By all means—she's a good customer, and a fine-spoken woman—and a woman who drinks and talks so freely will enliven the conversation.

PEACHUM: (*to the servant*) Desire her to walk in. (*The servant goes off to the right.*)

Scene Six

Mrs. Diana Trapes saunters in from the right. Her ponderous body is propelled forward with a gently rolling motion, making her look much like a drunken old sailor whose feet hurt. Her hair straggles out in all directions from beneath a dingy lace mobcap. Her faded blue dress, which might have been stolen from the wardrobe of a noble lady, is soiled and hangs awry. Her eyes are bleary and watery, with heavy blue-black bags beneath them. There is a mole on the right of her squarish, masculine chin. She kisses Peachum wetly on the cheek.

PEACHUM: Dear Mrs. Dye, your servant—one may know by your kiss, that your gin is excellent.

MRS. TRAPES: I was always very curious [8] in my liquors.

LOCKIT: (*leering*) There is no perfumed breath like it. I have been long acquainted with the flavor of those lips—han't I, Mrs. Dye? (*He holds a bottle and a glass and in pantomime offers her a drink.*)

MRS. TRAPES: Fill it up.—I take as large draughts of liquor as I did of love.—I hate a flincher in either.

AIR XLVI—A shepherd kept sheep, etc.

In the days of my youth I could bill like a dove, fa, la, la, etc.
Like a sparrow at all times was ready for love, fa, la, la, etc.
The life of all mortals in kissing should pass,
Lip to lip while we're young—then lip to the grass, fa la, etc.

(*wiping her mouth with the sleeve of her dress*) But now, Mr. Peachum, to our business.—If you have blacks of any kind, brought in of late; mantoes— [9] velvet scarfs—petticoats—let it be what it will, I am your chap—for all my ladies are very fond of mourning.

PEACHUM: Why look ye, Mrs. Dye—you deal so hard with us, that we can afford to give the gentlemen who venture their lives for the goods, little or nothing.

MRS. TRAPES: (*pausing to take a long, noisy drink and tapping herself on the chest with her fist as the liquor goes down past her bronchial tubes*) The hard times oblige me to go very near in my dealing. To be sure, of late years I have been a great sufferer by the parliament.—Three thousand pounds would hardly make amends.—The act for destroying the Mint [10] was a severe cut upon our business—till then, if a customer stepped out of the way—we knew where to have her. No doubt you know Mrs. Coaxer—there's a wench now (till to-day) with a good suit of clothes of mine upon her back, and I could never set eyes upon her for three months together. Since the act, too, against imprisonment for small sums, my loss there too hath been very considerable; and it must be so, when a lady can borrow a handsome petticoat, or a clean gown, and I not have the least hank [11] upon her! And, o' my conscience, nowadays most ladies take a delight in cheating, when they can do it with safety!

(*She motions for another drink, and Lockit pours it.*)

PEACHUM: Madam, you had a handsome gold watch of us t'other day for seven guineas. Considering we must have our profit—to a gentleman upon the road, a gold watch will be scarce worth the taking.

MRS. TRAPES: Consider, Mr. Peachum, that watch was remarkable and not of very safe sale. If you have any black velvet scarfs—they are handsome winter wear, and take with most gentlemen who deal with my customers. 'Tis I that put the ladies upon a good foot. 'Tis not youth or beauty that fixes their price. The gentlemen always pay according to their dress, from half a crown to two guineas; and yet those hussies make nothing of bilking me. Then, too, allowing for accidents. —I have eleven fine customers now under the surgeon's hands; [12] what with fees and other expenses, there are great goings-out, and no comings-in, and not a farthing to pay for at least a month's clothing. We run great risks—great risks indeed.

PEACHUM: (*inquisitively*) As I remember, you said something just now of a Mrs. Coaxer.

MRS. TRAPES: Yes, sir. To be sure, I stripped her of a suit of my own clothes about two hours ago, and have left her as she should be, in her shift, with a lover of hers, at my house. She called him upstairs as he was going to Marybone in a hackney coach. And I hope, for her sake and mine, she will persuade the captain to redeem her, for the captain is very generous to the ladies.

(*At the mention of the word "captain," both Lockit and Peachum become suddenly alert.*)

LOCKIT: (*excitedly*) What captain?

MRS. TRAPES: (*proudly*) He thought I did not know him—an intimate acquaintance of yours, Mr. Peachum —only Captain Macheath—as fine as a lord.

PEACHUM: (*doing a little jig in his glee*) To-morrow, dear Mrs. Dye, you shall set your own price upon any of the goods you like. We have at least a dozen velvet scarfs, and all at your service. Will you give me leave to make you a present of this suit of nightclothes for your own wearing? (*He hands her a negligee of flimsy silk.*)—But are you sure it is Captain Macheath?

MRS. TRAPES: (*smiling and nodding her head wisely*) Though he thinks I have forgot him, nobody knows him better. I have taken a great deal of the captain's money in my time at second-hand, for he always loved to have his ladies well-dressed.

PEACHUM: (*smiling roguishly to himself*) Mr. Lockit and I have business with the captain—you understand me—and we will satisfy you for Mrs. Coaxer's debt.

LOCKIT: Depend upon it—we will deal like men of honor.

MRS. TRAPES: (*indifferently*) I don't enquire after your affairs—so whatever happens, I wash my hands on't. It hath always been my maxim, that one friend should assist another.—But if you please, I'll take one of the scarfs home with me. 'Tis always good to have something in hand.

Scene Seven

The scene is Newgate Prison, perhaps an hour later. Lucy, in great despair, is seated at a table.

LUCY: Jealousy, rage, love, and fear are at once

tearing me to pieces. How I am weatherbeaten and shattered with distresses!

AIR XLVII—One evening, having lost my way, etc.

> *I'm like a skiff on the ocean tossed,*
> *Now high, now low, with each billow borne;*
> *With her rudder broke, and her anchor lost,*
> *Deserted and all forlorn.*
> *While thus I lie rolling and tossing all night,*
> *That Polly lies sporting on seas of delight!*
> *Revenge, revenge, revenge,*
> *Shall appease my restless sprite.*

(*looking at a small vial of poison she holds in her hand*) —I have the ratsbane ready. I run no risk; for I can lay her death upon the gin, and so many die of that naturally that I shall never be called in question. But say I were to be hanged—I never could be hanged for anything that would give me greater comfort than the poisoning that slut.

(*Filch walks slowly in from the right, idly picking his teeth with a straw.*)

FILCH: Madam, here's our Miss Polly come to wait upon you.

LUCY: Show her in.

Scene Eight

Polly enters from the right and walks primly toward Lucy. She is quite composed and seems determined to be cool to Lucy.

LUCY: (*arising and showering Polly with artificial cordiality*) Dear madam, your servant. I hope you will pardon my passion when I was so happy to see you last. I was so overrun with the spleen, that I was perfectly out of myself. And really when one hath the spleen, everything is to be excused by a friend.

AIR XLVIII—Now Roger, I'll tell thee,
        because thou'rt my son, etc.
When a wife's in her pout
(As she's sometimes, no doubt);
The good husband, as meek as a lamb,
    Her vapors to still,
    First grants her her will,
And the quieting draught is a dram.
Poor man! And the quieting draught is a dram.

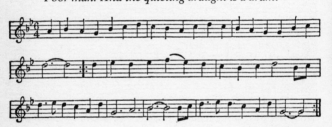

—I wish all our quarrels might have so comfortable a reconciliation.

POLLY: (*with chilly reserve*) I have no excuse for my own behavior, madam, but my misfortunes. And really, madam, I suffer too upon your account.

LUCY: (*sweetly*) But, Miss Polly—in the way of friendship, will you give me leave to propose a glass of cordial to you?

POLLY: (*unrelenting*) Strong waters are apt to give me the headache; I hope, madam, you will excuse me.

LUCY: (*enticingly*) Not the greatest lady in the land could have better in her closet, for her own private drinking.[13] You seem mighty low in spirits, my dear.

POLLY: (*haughtily*) I am sorry, madam, my health will not allow me to accept of your offer. I should not have left you in the rude manner I did when we met last, madam, had not my papa hauled me away so unexpectedly. I was indeed somewhat provoked, and perhaps might use some expressions that were disrespectful. But really, madam, the captain treated me with so much contempt and cruelty, that I deserved your pity, rather than your resentment.

LUCY: (*sadly*) But since his escape, no doubt, all matters are made up again.—Ah Polly! Polly! 'tis I am the unhappy wife, and he loves you as if you were only his mistress.

POLLY: (*warming before Lucy's sincerity*) Sure, madam, you cannot think me so happy as to be the object of your jealousy! A man is always afraid of a woman who loves him too well—so that I must expect to be neglected and avoided.

LUCY: Then our cases, my dear Polly, are exactly alike. Both of us, indeed, have been too fond.

AIR XLIX—O Bessy Bell

POLLY: *A curse attends that woman's love*
                     Who always would be pleasing.
LUCY: *The pertness of a billing dove,*
                     Like tickling, is but teasing.
POLLY: *What then in love can woman do?*
LUCY: *If we grow fond they shun us.*
POLLY: *And when we fly them, they pursue.*
LUCY: *But leave us when they've won us.*

LUCY: Love is so very whimsical in both sexes, that it is impossible to be lasting. But my heart is particular, and contradicts my own observations.

POLLY: (*consolingly*) But really, mistress Lucy, by his last behavior, I think I ought to envy you. When I was forced from him, he did not shew the least tenderness. But perhaps he hath a heart not capable of it.

AIR L—Would fate to me Belinda give.
Among the men, coquets we find,
Who court by turns all womankind;
And we grant all their hearts desired,
When they are flattered and admired.

The coquets of both sexes are self-lovers, and that is a love no other whatever can dispossess. I fear, my dear Lucy, our husband is one of those.

LUCY: Away with these melancholy reflections!—indeed, my dear Polly, we are both of us a cup too low. (*moving slowly toward the door*) Let me prevail upon you to accept of my offer.

AIR LI—Come, sweet lass, etc.
Come, sweet lass,
Let's banish sorrow
'Till to-morrow;
Come, sweet lass,
Let's take a chirping glass.
Wine can clear
The vapors of despair;
And make us light as air;
Then drink, and banish care.

I can't bear, child, to see you in such low spirits. And
I must persuade you to what I know will do you good.
(*aside to the audience as she goes out the door*) I shall
now be even with the hypocritical strumpet.

Scene Nine

POLLY: (*suspiciously*) All this wheedling of Lucy
cannot be for nothing—at this time too, when I know
she hates me!—The dissembling of a woman is always
the forerunner of mischief.—By pouring strong waters
down my throat, she thinks to pump some secret out of
me. I'll be upon my guard and won't taste a drop of
her liquor, I'm resolved.

Scene Ten

*Lucy returns from the right, carrying two glasses of
brandy.*

LUCY: (*gaily*) Come, Miss Polly.

POLLY: (*eying the glass questioningly*) Indeed, child,
you have given yourself trouble to no purpose.—You
must, my dear, excuse me.

LUCY: Really, Miss Polly, you are so squeamishly
affected about taking a cup of strong waters as a lady
before company. (*pushing the glass toward her*) I vow,
Polly, I shall take it monstrously ill if you refuse me.—
Brandy and men (though women love them never so
well) are always taken by us with some reluctance—
unless 'tis in private.

POLLY: (*picking up the glass unwillingly*) I protest,
madam, it goes against me. (*She sees something startling
off-stage to the right.*) What do I see! Macheath again
in custody!—Now every glimmering of happiness is lost.
(*She drops the glass of brandy.*)

LUCY: (*aside*) Since things are thus, I am glad the wench hath escaped: for by this event, 'tis plain, she was not happy enough to deserve to be poisoned.

Scene Eleven

Lockit, Peachum, and Macheath enter from the right. Macheath. his fine tarnished coat now removed and his hands chained behind him, does not struggle, but walks in with quiet dignity. Even in his simple white shirt he appears more elegantly dressed than the other men. Lockit and Peachum are obviously delighted with their catch.

LOCKIT: (*laughing cruelly*) Set your heart to rest, captain.—You have neither the chance of love, or money for another escape; for you are ordered to be called down upon your trial immediately.

(Polly and Lucy, both utterly distraught, kneel on either side of the captain and put their arms about his waist.)

PEACHUM: (*irately*) Away, hussies!—This is not a time for a man to be hampered with his wives. You see, the gentleman is in chains already.

LUCY: O husband, husband, my heart longed to see thee; but to see thee thus distracts me!

POLLY: Will not my dear husband look upon his Polly? Why hadst thou not flown to me for protection? With me thou hadst been safe.

AIR LII—The last time I went o'er the moor.

POLLY:	*Hither, dear husband, turn your eyes.*
LUCY:	*Bestow one glance to cheer me.*
POLLY:	*Think, with that look, thy Polly dies.*
LUCY:	*Oh shun me not—but hear me.*
POLLY:	*'Tis Polly sues.*
LUCY:	*—'Tis Lucy speaks,*
POLLY:	*Is thus true love requited?*
LUCY:	*My heart is bursting.*
POLLY:	*—Mine too breaks.*
LUCY:	*Must I?*
POLLY:	*—Must I be slighted?*

MACHEATH: (*tenderly*) What would you have me say, ladies?—You see, this affair will soon be at an end without my disobliging either of you.

PEACHUM: (*wrinkling his brow thoughtfully*) But the settling this point, captain, might prevent a lawsuit between your two widows.

MACHEATH: (*looking at Polly and Lucy alternately as he sings*)

AIR LIII—Tom Tinker's my true love.
Which way shall I turn me? How can I decide?
Wives, the day of our death, are as fond as a bride.
One wife is too much for most husbands to hear,
But two at a time there's no mortal can bear.
This way, and that way, and which way I will,
What would comfort the one, t'other wife would take ill.

POLLY: (*aside*) But if his own misfortunes have made him insensible to mine—a father sure will be more compassionate.—(*turning to Peachum*) Dear, dear sir, sink the material evidence, and bring him off at his trial! Polly upon her knees begs it of you.

AIR LIV—I am a poor shepherd undone.

When my hero in court appears,
* And stands arraigned for his life;*
Then think of poor Polly's tears;
* For ah! poor Polly's his wife.*
Like the sailor he holds up his hand,
* Distressed on the dashing wave.*
To die a dry death at land,
* Is as bad as a watery grave.*
* And alas, poor Polly;*
* Alack, and well-a-day!*
* Before I was in love,*
* Oh, every month was May!*

LUCY: (*crawling on her knees to Lockit*) If Peachum's heart is hardened, sure you, sir, will have more compassion on a daughter. I know the evidence is in your power. How can you be a tyrant to me?

AIR LV—Ianthe the lovely, etc.

When he holds up his hand arraigned for his life,
Oh, think of your daughter, and think I'm his wife!
What are cannons, or bombs, or clashing of swords?
For death is more certain by witnesses' words.
Then nail up their lips; that dread thunder allay;
And each month of my life will hereafter be May.

LOCKIT: (*unmoved*) Macheath's time is come, Lucy. We know our own affairs; therefore let us have no more whimpering or whining.

> *AIR LVI—A cobbler there was, etc.*
> *Ourselves, like the great, to secure a retreat,*
> *When matters require it, must give up our gang.*
>   *And good reason why,*
>   *Or instead of the fry,[14]*
>   *Even Peachum and I,*
> *Like poor petty rascals, might hang, hang;*
> *Like poor petty rascals might hang.*

PEACHUM: (*bluntly*) Set your heart at rest, Polly. Your husband is to die to-day! therefore, if you are not already provided, 'tis high time to look about for another.—There's comfort for you, you slut.

LOCKIT: (*to Macheath*) We are ready, sir, to conduct you to the Old Bailey.

MACHEATH:

> *AIR LVII—Bonny Dundee.*
> *The charge is prepared; the lawyers are met,*
> *The judges all ranged (a terrible show!).*
> *I go, undismayed—for death is a debt,[15]*
> *A debt on demand. So, take what I owe.*
> *Then farewell, my love—dear charmers, adieu.*
> *Contented I die—'tis better for you.*
> *Here ends all dispute the rest of our lives,*
>   *For this way at once I please all my wives.*

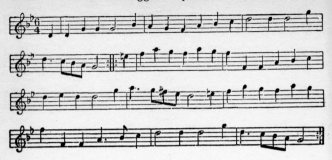

Now, gentlemen, I am ready to attend you.

Lockit and Peachum lead Macheath out to the right. As he goes out the door, the captain takes a farewell look at his two wives.

Scene Twelve

Filch wanders in from the left, apparently unaware of what has been going on.

POLLY: Follow them, Filch, to the court; and when the trial is over, bring me a particular account of his behavior, and of everything that happened.—You'll find me here with Miss Lucy.

(Filch, still somewhat puzzled, hurries out to the right. Sounds of music and boisterous revelry are heard off-stage.)

But why is all this music?

LUCY: The prisoners whose trials are put off till next sessions are diverting themselves.

POLLY: Sure there is nothing so charming as music! I'm fond of it to distraction! But alas! now, all mirth seems an insult upon my affliction.—Let's retire, my dear Lucy, and indulge our sorrows.—The noisy crew, you see, are coming upon us. *(Polly and Lucy go out to the left as the dancing prisoners burst upon the stage from the right.)*

The prisoners are an unbelievably motley crew as they prance and dance on stage. Some are dressed in high fashion, while others are covered in the most tat-

tered of rags. *All wear chains on their wrists. The dance is savage and yet somehow child-like; some of the more athletic prisoners leap upon the table and dance jigs, roughly pushing off others who try to join them. The dance goes on for several minutes until some of the prisoners skip off stage to the right, and the rest follow.*

Scene Thirteen

The scene is the condemned hold, perhaps a half hour later. Macheath is seated on the prison bunk in a melancholy posture. He holds a bottle of wine in his hand, and there are several more bottles of wine and liquor on the floor at his feet.

AIR LVIII—Happy groves.
O cruel, cruel, cruel case!
Must I suffer this disgrace?

AIR LVIX—Of all the girls that are so smart.
Of all the friends in time of grief,
When threatening death looks grimmer,
Not one so sure can bring relief,
As this best friend, a brimmer.

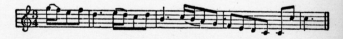

(He takes a long swig of wine.)

AIR LX—Britons, strike home.
Since I must swing,—I scorn, I scorn to wince or whine.

(He rises from the bunk and looks out the small cell window.)

AIR LXI—Chevy Chase.
But now again my spirits sink;
I'll raise them high with wine.

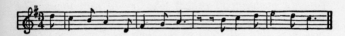

(*He takes another long, gurgling drink.*)

AIR LXII—To old Sir Simon the king.
But valor the stronger grows,
The stronger liquor we're drinking.
And how can we feel our woes,
When we've left the trouble of thinking?

(*He drinks again.*)

AIR LXIII—Joy to great Cæsar.
If thus—a man can die.
Much bolder with brandy.

(*He pours out a bumper of brandy.*)

AIR LXIV—There was an old woman.
So I drink off this bumper.—And now I can stand the test.
And my comrades shall see that I die as brave as the best.

(*He gulps the brandy down quickly.*)

AIR LXV—Did you ever hear of a gallant sailor.
> *But can I leave my pretty hussies,*
> *Without one tear, or tender sigh?*

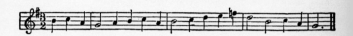

AIR LXVI—Why are mine eyes still overflowing.
> *Their eyes, their lips, their busses,*[16]
> *Recall my love.—Ah, must I die?*

AIR LXVII—Green sleeves.
> *Since laws were made for every degree,*
> *To curb vice in others, as well as me,*
> *I wonder we han't better company,*
> > *Upon Tyburn tree!*
> *But gold from law can take out the sting;*
> *And if rich men like us were to swing,*
> *'Twould thin the land, such numbers to string*
> > *Upon Tyburn tree!*

(*A jailor enters. He tips his three-cornered hat respectfully to the captain and unlocks the cell door to admit Ben Budge and Matt of the Mint.*)

JAILOR: Some friends of yours, captain, desire to be admitted.—I leave you together. (*The jailor locks the cell door and walks briskly off stage.*)

Scene Fourteen

Macheath gestures for Ben and Matt to sit on the bunk; he remains standing by the window.

MACHEATH: For my having broke prison, you see, gentlemen, I am ordered immediate execution. The sheriff's officers, I believe, are now at the door. That Jemmy Twitcher should peach me, I own, surprised me! 'Tis a plain proof that the world is all alike, and that even our gang can no more trust one another than other people. Therefore, I beg you, gentlemen, look well to yourselves, for in all probability you may live some months longer.

MATT: (*stoically*) We are heartily sorry, captain, for your misfortune.—But 'tis what we must all come to.

MACHEATH: Peachum and Lockit, you know, are infamous scoundrels. Their lives are as much in your power, as yours are in theirs. Remember your dying friend!—'Tis my last request. Bring these villains to the gallows before you, and I am satisfied.

MATT: (*loyally*) We'll do't.

(*The jailor re-enters and unlocks the cell.*)

JAILOR: Miss Polly and Miss Lucy entreat a word with you.

(*Polly and Lucy enter the cell as Ben and Matt go out.*)

MACHEATH: (*fondly*) Gentlemen, adieu.

(*The jailor locks the cell and goes out with Matt and Ben to the right.*)

Scene Fifteen

MACHEATH: (*spreading out his arms to embrace both the women*) My dear Lucy—my dear Polly! Whatsoever hath passed between us is now at an end. If you are fond of marrying again, the best advice I can give you is to ship yourselves off for the West Indies, where

you'll have a fair chance of getting a husband apiece—
or by good luck, two or three, as you like best.

POLLY: (*tearfully*) How can I support this sight!

LUCY: (*aside*) There is nothing moves one so much
as a great man in distress.

AIR LXVIII—All you that must take a leap, etc.

LUCY: *Would I might be hanged!*

POLLY: *—And I would so too!*

LUCY: *To be hanged with you.*

POLLY: *—My dear, with you.*

MACHEATH: *Oh, leave me to thought! I fear! I doubt!*
             I tremble! I droop!—See, my courage is
             out.

(*He turns up an empty bottle.*)

POLLY: *No token of love?*

MACHEATH: *—See, my courage is out.*

(*He turns up an empty wine pot.*)

LUCY: *No token of love?*

POLLY: *Adieu.*

LUCY: *Farewell!*

MACHEATH: *But hark! I hear the toll of the bell!*

CHORUS: *Tol de rol lol, etc.*

Keogh

(*The jailor enters from the right with a harried look on his face.*)

JAILOR: Four women more, captain, with a child apiece! See, here they come.

(*The jailor points to four fashionably dressed ladies of the town, each with a child of approximately a year old on her right hip. The women approach the cell door, all having the same expression of disdain on their faces.*)

MACHEATH: (*burying his face in his hands*) What —four wives more!—This is too much.—Here, tell the sheriff's officers I am ready.

(*The jailor takes Macheath off to the right, through the six irate women.*)

Scene Sixteen

The Player and the Beggar, dressed as before, enter from the left and stand at that end of the stage, watching the women in the center of the stage.

PLAYER: But, honest friend, I hope you don't intend that Macheath shall be really executed.

BEGGAR: Most certainly, sir. To make the piece perfect, I was for doing strict poetical justice. Macheath is to be hanged; and for the other personages of the drama, the audience must have supposed they were all either hanged or transported.

PLAYER: Why then, friend, this is a downright deep tragedy. The catastrophe is manifestly wrong, for an opera must end happily.

BEGGAR: Your objection, sir, is very just, and is easily removed; for you must allow that in this kind of drama, 'tis no matter how absurdly things are brought about. (*He spots one of the prisoners off-stage to the left; he claps his hands to get his attention.*) So—you rabble there! run and cry a reprieve!—let the prisoner be brought to his wives in triumph!

(*The rabble, a happy tatterdemalion, runs across the stage and disappears to the right.*)

PLAYER: All this we must do, to comply with the taste of the town.

BEGGAR: Through the whole piece you may observe

such a similitude of manners in high and low life, that
it is difficult to determine whether (in the fashionable
vices) the fine gentlemen imitate the gentlemen of the
road, or the gentlemen of the road the fine gentlemen.
Had the play remained as I at first intended, it would
have carried a most excellent moral. 'Twould have
shown that the lower sort of people have their vices
in a degree as well as the rich, and that they are
punished for them.

Scene Seventeen

*Macheath, surrounded by scores of laughing and
shouting rabble and all of the rest of the cast, enters
from the right. The captain silences the mob with a
wave of his hand before he speaks.*

MACHEATH: So it seems I am not left to my choice,
but must have a wife at last.—Look ye, my dears, we
will have no controversy now. Let us give this day to
mirth, and I am sure she who thinks herself my wife
will testify her joy by a dance.

ALL: Come, a dance—a dance!

MACHEATH: (*joyfully*) Ladies, I hope you will give
me leave to present a partner to each of you. (*walking
over to Polly and taking her arm*) And (if I may without offence) for this time, I take Polly for mine. (*to
Polly*) And for life, you slut, for we were really married.
As for the rest—but at present keep your own secret.
(*He motions for various members of the cast to take
the women as partners, and a wild, rambunctious parody
of the cotillion begins as Macheath sings.*)

> *AIR LXIX—Lumps of pudding, etc.*
> *Thus I stand like the Turk, with his doxies around;*
> *From all sides their glances his passion confound:*
> *For black, brown, and fair, his inconstancy burns,*
> *And the different beauties subdue him by turns.*
> *Each calls forth her charms, to provoke his desires;*
> *Though willing to all, with but one he retires.*
> *But think of this maxim, and put off your sorrow,*
> *The wretch of to-day may be happy to-morrow.*

CHORUS:
> *But think of this maxim, etc.*

FOOTNOTES

INTRODUCTION

[1] St. Giles is the patron saint of beggars; hence the outskirts of cities are often called "St. Giles."
[2] Songs.
[3] He lives by acting in the works of men who are inspired by the muses.
[4] This is an allusion to a famous contemporary quarrel between two operatic divas, Cuzzoni and Faustina.

ACT ONE

[1] The titles are the original names (or first lines) of the ballads and songs adapted by Gay.
[2] Gay's division of scenes follows the tradition in which each scene represents a changed situation, usually introduced by the entrance of a character or characters not on stage in the preceding scene. The parentheses indicate that no actual change of place occurs.
[3] He refers to the practice of pleading pregnancy to avoid being executed.
[4] Since Peachum is a "fence," his lock, or office, is a depot for stolen goods.
[5] Besides the usual meaning of the word the Augustans had two other meanings: one who collects taxes was a "customer" (Act I, scene iii) and a prostitute was a "customer" (Act III, scene vi).
[6] Newgate Prison.
[7] This refers to sessions of the criminal court.
[8] In his duties as a highway robber.
[9] The hangman's cart.
[10] These five names are references to the prime minister, Sir Robert Walpole. Bagshot refers to Bagshot Heath, a notorious haunt of robbers.
[11] Military service.
[12] An infamous London gambling resort.

[13] The Temple is the section of London where the Inns of Court (Inner and Middle Temple) are located.

[14] An abbreviated form of the word *chapman,* meaning customer.

[15] The dock section of London.

[16] A reference to the mode of punishing young delinquents by holding them under the public pump.

[17] Hockley-in-the-Hole was the scene of such gory sports as bear-baiting.

[18] London's criminal court.

[19] The report of confession, written by the prison chaplain.

[20] The flower market section of London.

[21] An older spelling of "cucumber."

[22] A town north of London.

[23] A clay-like substance used in filtering out impurities.

[24] In Gay's time the slang word *nim* meant "to steal."

[25] A jointure was a property settled on a woman by her spouse after his death.

[26] To peach is to inform against or to indict; this practice gave Peachum his descriptive name.

[27] His strategy and tactics in robberies on the highway.

[28] This is a notoriously impoverished district lying between Newgate Prison and the gallows at Tyburn.

[29] The gallows.

[30] A name given to all hangmen. In the seventeenth century there was an actual hangman of this name.

ACT TWO

[1] Skeletons.

[2] *Rinaldo* is the title of one of Handel's operas.

[3] This is a pun on the pseudo-science of alchemy, which sought to turn base metals into gold.

[4] A section of London inhabited largely by prostitutes.

[5] Hockley-in-the-Hole, Vinegar Yard, and Lewkner's Lane were places frequented by underworld characters.

[6] Merchants who sold on credit.

[7] A turtle-dove.

[8] From *Twelfth Night,* the first line of the play.

[9] Textile merchants.

[10] Two extremely expensive fabrics.

[11] Gaze.

[12] Translated from Augustan slang, Mrs. Vixen means that the apprentices spend lavishly ("bleed freely") of their masters' money and are thus deported.

[13] Sou, a small coin.

[14] When Lockit asks for garnish, he is asking for fees; the prisoners were given treatment in accord with the amount they paid the prison keeper.

[15] The prison chaplain.

[16] The government is "in arrears"; that is, it has not paid the rewards promised for the capture of criminals.

[17] Official position.

[18] Cheated.

[19] To trepan is to deceive.

ACT THREE

[1] Dupes.

[2] After casting its roe, a herring is thin and scrawny.

[3] "Setting upon," or robbing.

[4] A roll of coins.

[5] The account of the items stolen from the crowd at the coronation of George II in 1727.

[6] Train.

[7] A gudgeon is a type of fish easily caught by anglers; therefore the word came to mean any kind of "dupe."

[8] Particular or discriminating.

[9] Manteaus; loose robes or negligees.

[10] Southwark Mint was a favorite meeting place of criminals.

[11] Control.

[12] For either pre-natal care or the treatment of venereal diseases.

[13] During the eighteenth century fashionable women liked to pretend that they drank nothing stronger than wine.

[14] Small fish, or "small fry."

[15] Originally, the words *death* and *debt* were pronounced

alike. In *I Henry IV*, Act V, scene i, when the Prince says to Falstaff, "thou owest God a death," a similar pun is intended.

[16] Kisses.

BIBLIOGRAPHY

Sven M. Armens, *John Gay, Social Critic*. New York: King's Crown Press, 1954.

Frederick S. Boas, *An Introduction to Eighteenth-Century Drama, 1700–1780*. London: Oxford University Press, 1953.

Bertrand H. Bronson, *Studies in the Comic*. University of California Publications in English, vol. 8, no. 2, Berkeley and Los Angeles: University of California Press, 1941.

Donald Brook, *The Romance of the English Theatre*. London: Rockliff Co., 1952.

William Empson, *English Pastoral Poetry*. New York: W. W. Norton & Co., 1938.

G. C. Faber, ed., *The Poetical Works of John Gay*. London: Oxford University Press, 1926.

Edmond McAdoo Gagey, *Ballad Opera*. New York: Columbia University Press, 1937.

A. P. Herbert, *Mr. Gay's London*. London: Ernest Benn, Ltd., 1949.

Glenn Hughes, *The Story of the Theatre*. New York: Samuel French, 1938.

Leo Hughes, *A Century of English Farce*. Princeton: Princeton University Press, 1956.

William Henry Irving, *John Gay: Favorite of the Wits*. Durham, N.C.: Duke University Press, 1940.

———, *John Gay's London*. Cambridge: Harvard University Press, 1928.

Frank Kidson, *The Beggar's Opera: Its Predecessors and Successors*. London: Cambridge University Press, 1922.

John Clyde Loftis, *Comedy and Society from Congreve to Fielding*. Stanford: Stanford University Press, 1959.

James J. Lynch, *Box, Pit, and Gallery: Stage and Society in Johnson's London*. Berkeley and Los Angeles: University of California Press, 1953.

Karl Mantzius, *A History of Theatrical Art* (6 vols.). New York: Peter Smith Co., 1937.

Allardyce Nicoll, *The Development of the Theatre*. London: George G. Harrap & Co., Ltd., 1927.

———, *A History of Early Eighteenth-Century Drama, 1700–1750*. Cambridge: Cambridge University Press, 1929.

William E. Schultz, *Gay's Beggar's Opera*. New Haven: The Yale University Press, 1923.

Oscar Sherwin, *Mr. Gay*. New York: The John Day Co., 1929.

Richard Southern, *The Georgian Playhouse*. London: Pleiades Books Ltd., 1948.

James Sutherland, "John Gay" in *Eighteenth-Century English Literature: Modern Essays in Criticism,* James L. Clifford, ed. New York: Oxford University Press, 1959.

Fairfax P. Walkup, *Dressing the Part: A History of Costume for the Theatre*. New York: F. S. Crofts & Co., 1945.

A. W. Ward, *A History of English Dramatic Literature* 3 vols.). London: MacMillan & Co., Ltd., 1899.